To:- Ally
With

Thorburn's Wildlife

Frontispiece The common dormouse *Muscardinus avellanarius*

Dormouse. 3/4.

Thorburn's Wildlife

Jeremy Cardew

Windward

Thorburn's Wildlife

Jeremy Cardew

Illustrations by Archibald Thorburn. The sketches first published in 1919 in *A Naturalist's Sketchbook* are reproduced by kind permission of The Tryon Gallery. Illustrations first published in 1915–18 in *British Birds* and in 1920–1 in *British Mammals* are © George Rainbird Limited.

Reprinted 1982

Published in the UK by Windward an imprint owned by
W. H. Smith & Son Limited
Registered No. 237811 England
Trading as W.H.S. Distributors, St. John's House, East Street,
Leicester LE1 6NE

ISBN 0 7112 0027 0

Printed by Dai Nippon Printing Company Limited, Hong Kong

Contents

Introduction

Archibald Thorburn has long been recognized as one of the foremost natural history illustrators of the nineteenth century, and his popularity is reflected in the steady stream of posthumous publications of his illustrations. Well over one hundred works and publications bear witness to his talent for illustrating birds and mammals. But Thorburn was not just an illustrator; he was also a famous artist, commissioned to paint many canvases for the hunting and shooting fraternity. He particularly excelled in the portrayal of game-birds and the wildlife of the Scottish Highlands. Above all, he was an individualist, depicting for the first time British birds and mammals as they appear in their natural environment. Moreover, unlike many earlier illustrators, he did not allow his preoccupation with scientific detail to detract from the artistic quality of his paintings.

The son of Robert Thorburn, miniaturist painter to Queen Victoria, Archibald Thorburn enjoyed excellent coaching in fine arts. He inherited a keen interest in natural history from his grandfather, Prideaux John Selby, the famous Victorian naturalist. Educated in his native Edinburgh and in Dalkeith, he was sent to art school in St. John's Wood, London. 1883 saw the publication of his first sketches in J. E. Harting's *Sketches of Bird Life*. He then worked on numerous plates for Swaysland's *Familiar Wild Birds* over the next five years. At the age of 26 he was employed to illustrate Lord Lilford's *Coloured Figures of the Birds of the British Islands* because illness had overtaken J. G. Keulemans, the resident artist. During the following 13 years Thorburn produced over half the 500 plates needed for this monumental work which established his reputation.

All these early plates were reproduced by hand. Originals were drawn in wax on a lithographic plate, from which a limited number of prints could be made. The development of modern

Wild white cattle *Bos taurus*. Of uncertain origin, these 'wild' cattle are now considered to be descended from escaped domestic animals which sheltered for some years in forests before being rounded up in medieval times. They became localized as land was cleared, and now are best seen in parks like Cadzow and Chartley.

printing processes over the following 20 years revolutionized the production of colour plates and the new four-colour photographic process replaced the old method. The durability of the new printing plates brought about a hundred-fold increase in production. This rendered the reproduction of colour plates in books cheaper and, consequently, more accessible to the general public. Thus, a new generation of naturalists were inspired who, equipped with bicycles or even motorcars, began to take an interest in the wildlife of the surrounding countryside.

Thorburn's style of painting is highly original, showing little or no influence of contemporary artists. Instead of dwelling on the detail of every individual feather, he captures a realistic impression of the living animal without sacrificing accuracy. In so doing, he manages to combine artistic flair with scientific precision. His Swedish contemporary, Bruno Liljefors, regarded Thorburn as an excellent Impressionist, on a par with the American painter Audubon of the early 1800s.

Notes and sketches always played an important role in Thorburn's methods. Simple pencil sketches caught the natural stances and form of his subject, while the beautiful but simple watercolour sketches provided accurate information on the plumage and body colour. Live specimens in zoos and private collections were as important to Thorburn as those in the wild, for many of the species he illustrated were extremely rare, or even extinct, in Britain. Private and museum collections of skins were sometimes used to provide fine detail of the animals and birds. Of the many thousands of sketches he made, the best were selected for his *Naturalist's Sketchbook*, published in 1919. A few of those sketches are included in this book.

The new printing processes allowed artists freedom in the choice of medium for their original paintings. Thorburn mainly used guache and watercolour. This gave a depth of colour and fineness of detail to his later paintings not possible in earlier chromolithography and engravings. The publication of *British Birds* in 1915 and *British Mammals* five years later came when Thorburn was at the height of his career.

This present book reproduces a selection of plates from the three volumes and highlights the diversity of his talent. The composition of many plates reveals the thoroughness of his observations. Details of habitat are conveyed in a subtle way, for example by the inclusion of some plant closely associated with the same habitat as the animal illustrated: thrift with the gulls, and stonecrop with the wallcreeper for example.

On occasions, Thorburn the artist takes over from Thorburn the scientist, however, as with his obsession with the colourful plumage of the male bird. Nearly always the comparatively drab female is relegated to the background, while the male dominates the foreground. This is especially noticeable in the blackbird, the ducks and the gamebirds. But this criticism does not detract from the value of his work.

In *British Birds*, the organization of the birds in the plates does not always correspond with present-day views on the separation of bird groups. Scientific nomenclature has changed in the past, and will probably change in the future. Thorburn's plates are, however, still useful to the naturalist; indeed today's naturalist will find many of the illustrations comparable in accuracy with the best now available in field guides, and as delightful to the eye as past generations of art and nature lovers have done.

Thorburn did not include measurements of scale in his sketches and colour plates of birds. A general impression of size may be interpreted from the plants illustrated. The mammals on Thorburn's original plates, from *British Mammals* (1920–1), were drawn reduced in size. Some of these plates have a scale number beside the species name. These scales refer to the original plates which have been reduced by about a third for reproduction in this edition.

Gyrfalcon *Falco rusticolus*. These two subspecies depict the two most typical colour phases found in Greenland (left) and Iceland (right). Both birds are males. The species are annual vagrants to Scotland and England, usually in winter and spring. The Greenland variety is the more common.

Pl.

Brown Rat. 2/3.

Wildlife and Man

Man has affected the wildlife of Britain in a variety of ways. Firstly he has been an important agency in the establishment of alien mammals and birds in Britain. The accidental introduction of rats and mice has at various times in history wreaked havoc among the population, causing death through starvation and the disease 'black death'. Another introduced rodent is the grey squirrel, brought from America. Deer, gamebirds and rabbits were imported by the Normans in the eleventh and twelfth centuries to provide food and sport. Many other introductions and escapes of alien species have occurred, and some are now regarded as members of the British fauna. Man's activities have been responsible for the extinction of many species, but the historic protection of game has enabled some of the ancient woodlands and forests to survive the vagaries of agriculture and industry over the centuries, and the retention of woods, copses and parks for game has provided some habitat security for the indigenous wildlife.

Rats

More loss of life and destruction of communities has been caused by the black rat *Rattus rattus* than by any other mammal in man's history. A native of the forests of southeast Asia, this insidious rodent was claimed to have been brought in inadvertently by the Holy War crusaders of the Middle Ages on their return from the Levant. It spread throughout Europe and caused much damage to stored crops and materials, but made its greatest impact by the transmission of the bubonic plague. Between a third and a quarter of the population of Europe died from the Black Death in the fourteenth century. These plagues continued to ravage humanity, often carried to unsuspecting regions by mercenary armies, and culminated in Britain in the Great Plague of London in 1665. Even now viable bacteria are found in the soils of 300-year-

The brown or common rat *Rattus norvegicus* is generally stouter than the black rat, and has a rounder head and muzzle, smaller ears and a comparatively shorter and more scaly tail.

old plague burial pits when they are inadvertently opened during building operations. The Isle of North Rona had a thriving population in the 1600s which became extinct because black rats, which had been introduced accidentally, destroyed the islanders' winter food supplies.

Unlike the brown rat, the black rat lives predominantly above ground, in the caves and walls of buildings, and in thatch and trees in warm climates. The British distribution in inland towns and villages has severely contracted over the last two centuries. The black rat's strongholds are still the ports and cities where it feeds on stores of agricultural products, especially fruits and grains.

The decline of the black rat has been counterbalanced by the spread throughout Europe of the brown or common rat *Rattus norvegicus*. This rat grows larger than the black rat and is easily distinguished by its general brown colour, shorter muzzle and thicker, shorter tail. It is commonly associated with water, and in rivers and ponds is often mistaken for the water vole. But it is equally at home in sewers, sewage farms, buildings and farms. When there is an abundant supply of food, these rats will live side by side, the brown rat mainly below ground, the black above. But where there is competition for food and space, the brown rat will kill and even eat its relative, a common occurrence in the Americas and Israel where the brown rat population is expanding into black rat domains. Being less of a vegetarian, the brown rat causes damage and destruction to a greater range of man's goods than the black rat ever did. Leather shoes can be eaten and concrete and lead pipes do not inhibit its burrowing habits. Like the house mouse, the rats used to inflict heavy losses on stored cereal products, but the widespread use of steel silos and reinforced concrete farm buildings have diminished their impact in developed nations. However, some third world countries still lose up

The black rat *Rattus rattus* is a smaller and leaner animal than the common rat. Illustrated here are two races, the Alexandrine rat and the 'old English black rat' or Northern Alexandrine rat. A third, the black Alexandrine rat which has a jet black, glossy coat, was described as a recent arrival.

Pl. 29
A. Thorburn 1919.
rine Rat. Black Rat. $\frac{2}{3}$

The common or house mouse *Mus musculus*. This worldwide species is distinguishable from other mice by its tail which is thicker and more prominently scaly. It has an excellent sense of balance and considerable climbing ability.

to a third of their stored foods in this way. Since brown rats are not wholly dependent on human habitation, many survive in fields during summer and autumn, returning after harvest time to the security and plentiful supply of food in the barns and haystacks.

Man's everlasting war against this most hated of pests has witnessed the development of chemicals for its control. Widespread use of the rat poison *Warfarin* was at first successful, but now many incidences of resistance and avoidance behaviour to this bait have been recorded and have fostered the super-rat of science fiction. The destruction of foods, and their contamination by rat droppings, hair and possibly disease, still makes this pest an important economic factor throughout the world.

The spread of the brown rat across Europe took only a few decades. Russian ships brought it to Denmark in 1716, Ireland in 1722 and from these three countries it arrived in Britain between 1728 and 1730. Scotland was still being colonized in the 1850s and America in the 1950s. The ravages of this rodent are such that numerous deaths from their attack have been recorded. They were once thought to be venomous as their bite caused severe infections in many patients.

House Mouse

It was perhaps the Neolithic migrations of man 4000 to 5000 years ago that brought the ubiquitous house mouse *Mus musculus* to Europe. The secrets of man's prerecorded history are now coming to light with modern investigations into Neolithic settlements, and house mouse remains from such a settlement in Dorset confirm that the association of man and mouse is indeed ancient. Its adaptability to man's environment is considerable, and continues. Mice are found down coalmines, where they live in perpetual darkness on the waste of men and horses, and even in the arctic conditions of meat coldstores. In London's Smithfield market such mice feed on frozen meat and have developed long, thick pelts. But still the majority are found around inhabited buildings, warehouses and farms, although in summer substantial populations are also encountered in the hedgerows and banks of the countryside. Little is known of these ferals except that they probably derive from farm mice and never seem to outnumber the resident wood mice and bank voles; their main predators are stoats, weasels and barn owls. The importance of domestic cats as controllers of house mice is generally overrated; they probably only destroy mice moving in the open and between buildings. In towns, man and the brown rat remain the chief predators.

Improvements and changes in agricultural practices and sanitary conditions have reduced the effect on man of this destructive little rodent. Nowadays it is usually considered no more than a nuisance. Before the last war wheat was mainly stored unthreshed in ricks and this abundant food supply and protected breeding environment provided farm mice with all their needs. A breeding rate of ten litters a year was possible, with five to six young per litter. Thus an accumulation of 2000 mice in a single rick was not uncommon, and when evicted during threshing the resultant spray of mice caused considerable inconvenience. In residential accommodation, with the comparative sparsity of food and nesting sites, house mice produce only five to six litters per year. Their extermination has been aided by pest-control officers employed by local authorities, but total eradication from rambling dwellings may be impossible.

Mice can mate directly after birth of a litter, but implantation of the fertilized eggs is then delayed by two to sixteen days. Gestation takes twenty days and the young are weaned at two to three weeks. In a fast-breeding population, female juveniles become sexually mature at six weeks, but when the population reaches medium densities the rate of breeding declines as does the number of young in a litter. At very high densities breeding may cease altogether. Such attributes are exhibited by most of the other rodent species, especially rats and voles.

Investigations into the potential of mice as reservoirs and transmitters of diseases have been inadequate up to now. Their importance as carriers of *Leptospira*, *Rickettsia* and *Salmonella* bacteria, transmitted by the mouse-parasitic fleas and lice, has not yet been determined, but is probably decreasing with the improvements in household sanitary conditions and legal provisions for rodent control.

Many races and subspecies of the house mouse have been described, the most famous being the St Kilda house mouse *M. musculus muralis*. This differs from the western European and British *M. m. domesticus* by being larger in body and with a paler-coloured belly, and from the Scandinavian and eastern European *M. m. musculus* which is darker. The St Kilda house mouse has been found only on the island of Hirta off the northwest coast of Scotland and was always associated with the cottages and cleits of the isle. When the island was evacuated in 1930, individual mice survived in only two of the cottages where food stores were still present. By 1931 only a couple of dozen mice were left and by 1938 even these had gone. In contrast, the St Kilda wood mouse *Apodemus sylvaticus* var. *hirtensis* spread from the lowland fields into the house mice haunts and continued in these even after rehabilitation of the cottages by the military in 1958.

Deer

The history of the deer family in Britain is complicated and closely related to the history of man in these Isles. Prehistoric deer, such as the giant Irish fallow deer, and the reindeer *Rangifer tarandus* thrived on the tundra and boreal countryside after the last glaciation. Archaeological remains suggest that both had become extinct by the Bronze Age. Neolithic remains of the Irish fallow deer have been recorded from Stone Age cave sites in Cumbria, along with bones of reindeer and the short-horned Celtic ox. This giant fallow deer was the size of an elk, and although standing little over 200 centimeters at the shoulder, it carried outsize antlers: up to 490 centimetres across and weighing 75 kilograms. Although related to the fallow deer from Southern Europe it is not its ancestor in Britain. The reindeer was re-introduced into the Cairngorms from Scandinavia in 1952. This herd has thrived with only one addition, a Russian stag imported to strengthen the stock.

The red deer *Cervus elaphus* and roe deer *Capreolus capreolus* have inhabited Britain since the development, in Neolithic times, of broad-leaved forests where they browse on the foliage. The ancient English kings hunted these deer with arrows, nets and dogs. From Norman times, large tracts of land were converted into protected deer forests, and remnants of these have survived, namely the New Forest, Windsor Great Park, and Sherwood Forest. But in Scotland many of the old remaining forests were cut down by order, and the red deer established itself on the treeless moorlands. These deer have tended to become stockier and smaller than those remaining in the shelter of forests.

The need for hardwood timber from the sixteenth to eighteenth centuries resulted in massive clearances for shipbuilding, glass and pottery manufacture, so that by the end of the eighteenth

The fallow deer *Cervus dama* was kept by the Romans and spread across Europe with the Empire. Its introduction to Britain, however, is attributed to the Normans. Three forms are shown; the spotted summer form of the stag and hind, the creamy 'menil' race which lacks the rump markings, and the dark summer form of the 'dun'.

century, the lowlands were nearly devoid of deer haunts except in a few protected parks. Wild red deer and the smaller roe deer could only be found on the wilds of Exmoor, in the Lake District and in Scotland. Extensive afforestation in the nineteenth century allowed the re-introduction of the roe deer to southern England and East Anglia. Now they are commonly seen in dense woodlands from Essex to Cornwall.

The roe deer is usually solitary, although they may be seen in small groups. It emerges from the dense undergrowth of woodlands at night to feed in the open. In common with all British deer, other than the reindeer, only the male has antlers. These rarely grow to more than three points. Another conspicuous feature is the pale rump in winter.

The red deer has remained a popular game animal. Many were imported from European parks to supplement the British stocks, resulting in the characteristic different strains. Over the centuries, red deer in northern and western Europe have decreased in size. The huge stags of central Europe have disappeared from the German forests, where in the early and mid-seventeenth century, there are records of dressed weights of between 200 kilograms and 350 kilograms. These had diminished to 100 kilograms by the early 1900s. This decrease in deer weight has not occurred in eastern and southeastern European deer stocks.

In the deer forests of the uplands stalking is now controlled in order to keep deer stocks healthy and at economic levels. Without adequate control deer may do considerable damage to young trees by rubbing against them to remove the velvet from their antlers, and in severe winters hungry deer will strip the bark off trees.

The Manchurian Sika deer *Cervus nippon* is medium sized and faintly spotted in summer. It has become established in a dozen localities in

Roe deer *Capreolus capreolus* are native to broadleaved forests where they browse on the foliage. Smaller than red deer and usually solitary, they keep to the dense undergrowth of woodlands, emerging at night to feed in the open. Illustrated here are the fully grown antlers of the male, with a brow and two points.

Pl. 39.

Britain by escapes from parks. Though it is smaller than the red deer, up to 120 centimetres long in the adult as opposed to the 250 centimetres of the red deer, Sika stags sometimes mate with red hinds and produce a spotted and fertile hybrid. But the restricted distribution of the Sika at present means it has yet to threaten the purity of the red deer stock.

The fallow deer *Cervus dama* was kept by the Romans and spread with the expansion of the Empire throughout Europe. Its introduction to Britain is attributed, however, to the Normans. Further introductions have since been made, and escapes from open parks and estates have successfully colonized woodlands throughout Britain. Thorburn illustrates three forms: the spotted summer form of the stag and hind which were prevalent in most English parks during the seventeenth century; the pale creamy 'menil' race which lacks the dark markings on the rump; and the dark summer form of the 'dun', the deer introduced by the Normans to provide easily available venison.

Several other species have also been introduced to Britain. Two related species, the Chinese muntjac *Muntiacus reevesi* and the Indian muntjac *M. muntjac*, have been introduced at various times to deer parks, but only the Chinese species appears to have successfully adapted to feral life in the thick woodlands of the Midlands. It is very small, up to 100 centimetres long, deep red and unspotted. The males have a pair of slender tusks which protrude from the upper jaw and very short, simple antlers which project backwards from permanent stalks. Another small species, the Chinese water deer *Hydropotes inermis*, is very limited in distribution. It was introduced at Woburn, Bedfordshire, at the start of the twentieth century and can now be found in woodland and grassland in surrounding counties.

Opposite Male red deer *Cervus elaphus* with the fine branching antlers, and hinds in the background. They are usually found in groups.
Right Notes and sketches played an important role in Thorburn's methods. Pencil drawings such as these of red deer, caught the natural stances of his subjects.

Pheasants

The Greeks brought pheasants *Phasianus colchicus* to Athens from the Black Sea city of Colchis. The name pheasant derives from the river Phasis, also renowned from the expedition the Argonauts made to the area. The Romans eventually procured pheasants and began to farm them for food and decoration.

Although remains have been recovered from a Roman site in Britain, this bird was not permanently established until its introduction, along with fallow deer and rabbit, by the Normans and crusaders. Since then, it has supplied both meat and sport, first through netting and hawking and later by hounds and the gun. It is now one of our most popular gamebirds. Man's eternal desire for the improvement of game led first to the introduction of the Japanese pheasant *P. versicolor* in 1741, and then another race of *P. colchicus*, the large ring-necked or Mongolian pheasant, in the middle of the nineteenth century. These races and species of pheasant have interbred since, giving Britain the diversity of forms it has today.

The destructive habits of the pheasant have been equated to those of the woodpigeon, but their protection under the game laws affords them the immunity denied many other animals. The ancient Royal hunting laws for pheasants have now become the game laws of today, with the pheasant the most popular gamebird of the lowlands. Today hundreds of thousands are bred in enclosures and then released on to shooting land. This has limited the destruction of predators to the vicinity of these breeding enclosures and during the breeding season the disturbance of wildlife is reduced to a minimum. Increasing preoccupation with the shooting of 'cultivated' gamebirds such as pheasant, partridge and grouse, has eased the pressure on our wildlife, and the protection of copses, moors and hedgerows for the gamebirds has in turn provided secure habitats for many birds and mammals elsewhere at risk from the encroachment of agriculture and building.

Further introductions have been made even since Thorburn's time. Golden pheasants *Chrysolophus pictus* were locally introduced into parks and gardens, and now wild populations are found in such diverse areas as Kew Gardens, East Anglia and the Lake District. Escapes of Lady Amherst's pheasants *C. amherstiae* have also become permanent residents of the British wildlife around Woburn, along with the wallabies and Chinese water deer. In contrast, Reeve's pheasant *Syrmaticus reevesi* was introduced into the wilds of the Highlands, into Dorset and into the Grizedale Forest, Cumbria. With its two-metre-long tail it must rate as the most spectacular of all Britain's naturalized gamebirds.

Opposite Pheasants *Phasianus colchicus* were first established throughout Europe in Norman times. The feral stock shows the pattern of several wild races which have been used to refresh it: Mongolian pheasant (*top left*), Chinese ring-necked or grey rumped pheasant (*bottom left*), black-necked pheasant male (*middle*) and female (*bottom right*), and Japanese pheasant *P. versicolor* (*middle right*) which hybridizes with *P. colchicus*.
Left A study from a collection of pheasants in an aviary.

Mongolian Pheasant (♂ & ♀). Pheasant (♂ & ♀). Japanese Pheasant

Common Partridge. (♂ & ♀)
Red-legged Partridge. (♂ & ♀)
Quail. (♂ & ♀)

Partridges and Quails

The increase in importance of pheasants as gamebirds occurred mainly in response to the decline of grey partridges *Perdix perdix*. Over-hunting and bad weather since the 1600s were the probable cause of this decline but the resident game was exposed to even greater pressure as the development of the gun gradually replaced hawking.

After a hundred years of failure, the French or redlegged partridge *Alectoris rufa* was successfully established as a British gamebird in 1770. It has never extended its range naturally north of the Midlands but there have been recent introductions to Scotland and to the Isle of Man. The grey partridge, however, inhabits the whole British Isles. In the southern countries of England, the French partridge is regarded as a hardy bird capable of rearing healthy broods in the wet springs during which the native birds succumb to cold and starvation. Both species feed on insects, seeds, green leaves and split grain.

The advent of reaping and mowing machines since the turn of the century has taken its toll of young and eggs in the agricultural fields where the grey tends to make its nest. The French species is generally more closely associated with uncultivated lands of the lowlands and therefore is less prone to such destruction. Lately, the effect of insecticides and herbicides and the destruction of hedgerows has further restricted the food supply for the chicks in late spring, resulting in a more local distribution of the grey species.

The quail *Coturnix coturnix* is a small relative of the partridges, but is found in England only from May to October. Its migrations between the African winter and European summer grounds are widely recorded in the history of the Mediterranean region, providing as they did the major income for such small islands as Capri, as well as some of the islands of the Peloponnese. Captures of hundreds of thousands of these birds while on this migration route probably account for their diminishing numbers over the past 50 years. The changing climates of Europe and Africa may have contributed to their decline. Though now uncommon in Britain, it is still possible to flush this bird from its haunts in the open and rich, chalky lands of the Downs.

Opposite: The grey partridge *Perdix perdix* (*top*) is less colourful and smaller than the redlegged or French partridge *Alectoris rufa* (*bottom left*). The quail *Coturnix coturnix* (*bottom right*) is a smaller relative and a regular summer visitor.

Above left and right Studies of a partridge and quail.

The woodcock *Scolopax rusticola* (*top right*) is a bird of woodland where it rests camouflaged in deep cover. The common snipe *Gallinago gallinago* (*top left*) shown here in display-flight, great snipe *G. media* (*bottom right*) and jack snipe *Lymocryptes minimus* (*bottom left*) prefer the grasses and rushes of wetlands.

Woodcock and snipe

The flesh of the woodcock *Scolopax rusticola* is well known for its flavour and delicacy. Even in Charles II's time the following distich illustrating the importance of gamebirds in the history and culture of Britain, was in vogue:

> If the partridge had the woodcock's thigh,
> It would be the best bird that e'er did flit.

Four waders are still important as game. These are the woodcock, common snipe *Gallinago gallinago*, great snipe *G. media* and jack snipe *Lymocryptes minimus*. All four are recorded as passage migrants or winter residents, although resident populations of the woodcock and snipe breed in Britain. Their numbers are bolstered during the winter months by the migrants from the moors and tundra of northern Europe and Russia. The great snipe very rarely reaches British shores. The smallest snipe, the jack, has a shorter route. Whereas its summer haunts are similar to those of the great snipe, it winters in the wet moors, marshes and saltmarshes of Britain.

The three snipe are easily separated by size. The jack is only about 20 centimetres long while the others are closer to 30 centimetres. The great snipe has very noticeable patches of white on the lateral tail feathers; these are less obvious in the common and completely absent in the jack. Both the jack and the great have a slower and more direct flight and do not call when rising after being flushed. In France, the common snipe is called *'chèvre volant'* and in Scotland the 'heather bleater', both names due to the drumming or bleating sound made by the male during courtship displays. For many years the origin of this sound was unknown. It derives from the tail feathers splayed sideways which resonate as the bird dives. Thorburn illustrates this display-flight.

The common snipe is a widely spread species of both American continents and ranges from Europe to Japan, from the arctic to the Mediterranean. But the British numbers have steadily declined over the last 30 years possibly due to the disturbance and reclamation of its nesting areas, the wet moors, water-meadows and marshes.

All snipe have the characteristically shaped bill which is shorter in the jack and thicker in the woodcock. All have a flexible, sensitive and soft membraneous tip to the upper mandible which greatly increases the success with which they extract worms, snails and other invertebrates from the mud. The flexibility of the upper bill tip allows the tongue to draw in food without the bill being opened.

Unlike other snipe, the woodcock is a woodland bird, and is easily distinguished by the transverse black bars on its head, its greater size and stouter bill. It nests in dry, warm situations in deep cover, while the other snipes prefer coarse wetland grasses and rushes. Since the planting of woodlands in Scotland over the last 200 years woodcock numbers have increased dramatically. Its disruptive coloration camouflages the woodcock well against dead grass and leaves, and it counts on this camouflage until danger is imminent: only then does it take flight into the wind, keeping low among the trees.

Upland Wildlife

The mountains and moorlands of Britain remained relatively undisturbed by man until the 1800s. The poor soils were agriculturally uneconomic until the widespread establishment of upland sheep farming. Later development of vast hunting and shooting estates caused further disturbance to the wildlife, especially with the intense persecution of birds of prey and other predators. It is only the highest moors and mountains which have not yet been disturbed by man. But the recent increase in popularity of outdoor recreational pursuits – skiing, climbing and walking – are gradually encroaching on these habitats. National and local organizations are now playing an important part in the preservation of the uplands and their sub-arctic plants and wildlife.

Bustards

The great bustard *Otis tarda* received much attention from the early naturalists owing to its size and the male's mythical ability to store a gallon of water in its throat pouch. Many eminent people debated this theory which remained unresolved when the bird became locally extinct in the mid-eighteenth century. But it is known now that during courtship display the male blows up this pouch with air and, looking as though he has turned himself inside out, masquerades as a mass of white feathers. Attempts begun in the early 1970s to re-introduce it into its ancient haunts on Salisbury Plain are still in progress.

Once common on the plains and heaths of Norfolk, Suffolk and the Dorset uplands, flocks upwards of 50 strong would enjoy indolent security guarded by sentinel birds. These would watch the distant hedges and woods for any potential predators they sheltered, and only the fleetest of hounds had a chance of catching an adult bird. But the ever present demand for agricultural land encroached on the plains, and the advent of the long-range rifle took its toll on both the great and little bustards *Tetrax tetrax*. Only in remote and secluded mountain estates in Europe have flocks managed to survive; a number are still found in Majorca despite the tourist boom on the island.

Occasional vagrants from the Continent arrive in Britain, but these influxes are unlikely to result in natural recolonization. The success on Salisbury Plain is only possible in the undisturbed areas of Government-controlled land around Porton Down.

Opposite Two male great bustards *Otis tarda* displaying (*centre*), and one on sentinal duty (*right*). A pair of juvenile lapwings *Vanellus vanellus* are overhead.
Left Two sketches taken from a bustard in captivity with the throat pouch expanded and feathers furred-up during the courtship display.

Pl. 6

Great Bustard. (889.)

Pl.

Capercaillie (♂ & ♀)

Gamebirds

In contrast to the bustards, Britain's other large gamebird, the capercaillie *Tetrao urogallus* is fairly common throughout the Highlands of Scotland. The cock is easily distinguished from other members of the grouse family by his large size – close to that of an American turkey. Some cocks will attack people encroaching on their territory. Like many other grouse this species is boreal in distribution, and was probably a common bird over the whole of Britain when, after the last Ice Age, coniferous forests were extensive; it is now found throughout Europe in this habitat. By the end of the eighteenth century it had become extinct due to over-hunting, but Swedish stock introduced in the early 1800s was successful in recolonizing the Highlands. It is to be hoped that its strange love song will become common in the vast Forestry Commission Border forests where young birds have lately been introduced. These protected forests are now the homes of red squirrel, pine marten, birds of prey and the black grouse, and have played a large part in ensuring the survival of these species in Britain.

In early spring, pine forest clearings and glades are sites of the ritual breeding ceremonies of the male black grouse, or blackcock *Tetrao tetrix*, when the lyre-shaped tail of the male distinguishes him from other grouse. The provision of such areas in some planted woodlands has been possible with the cooperation of the Forestry Commission who realize that such diversity in man-made forests is of paramount importance for the survival of a wide range of wildlife.

Pine needles and young shoots are the most important food for the black grouse as for the capercaillie. Black grouse feed, court, and nest on the ground although in winter it is also arboreal. It was widespread throughout the whole of Britain until the nineteenth century but by the 1920s had gone from its strongholds in the southwest. It was then restricted from the Pennines northwards to Scotland, and to Wales, with only a few on Exmoor and the Quantocks. The tide of habitat destruction turned with the replanting of the coniferous woodlands for timber. It survives best where it can range into local moors and farmland for feeding. Unlike its counterpart the red grouse *Lagopus lagopus*, it was not favoured by the Victorian shooting fraternity for, when flushed from cover, it has the habit of running rather than flying.

The red grouse became so fashionable a bird for shooting that changes were made to many moorlands. In the Victorian Age, the society of hunting and shooting reached a zenith which drastically changed the face of the British uplands and their associated wildlife and flora. Instead of walking a good distance and picking a mixed bag of game, the fashion changed and the game was driven towards the guns. The grouse admirably suited this type of shooting and thus became famed for its sport. By eradication of all predators and careful management of heather, grouse numbers were increased greatly. Old heather moors were systematically burned to provide fresh growth for adult birds and adequate insect food for the chicks, and tall cover was kept to a maximum of 30 centimetres high. Old sheep-grazing lands were thus converted, and the celebration of the sport was repeated each year on the glorious twelfth (of August).

It was not until 1911 when a government commission reported on the state of the 'red grouse disease', that the effect of the farming of grouse on predators was fully appreciated. Wholesale slaughter of predators was the order of the day. The commission reported that:

> This philosophy relates to many of man's attempts at controlling 'nature' but without an understanding of the natural state of things and the effect on the natural wildlife. Indiscriminate killing of predators can lead to many unforeseen problems. For instance eagles and ravens would, if protected, help to keep down other corvids, stoats and weasels which have lately become prevalent.

The capercaillie *Tetrao urogallus* is the largest member of the grouse family. The male or cock (*top*) is a large turkey-like bird easily distinguished from the mottled brown female (*bottom*), the size of a hen pheasant. In early spring the male may be seen displaying its broad fan-tail in the northern pine forests.

But it is an ill wind that blows no good. More was known about this bird than about any other species, and the interest in its study had the effect of stimulating research into the lives of other birds, and probably helped to initiate the study of behavioural ecology. This marked trend in natural history, away from just noting occurrences and towards the study and understanding of the needs of different species, was greatly encouraged by the publication of reliable bird books in Thorburn's day. His illustrations, though often depicting only the most colourful forms, showed the birds in lifelike attitudes in the wild. This stimulated many a latent naturalist into activity at the very time when improved means of transport made the British countryside more accessible.

Opposite Red grouse *Lagopus lagopus* (*above*) in spring and the black grouse *Tetrao tetrix*, male or blackcock (*bottom right*) and female or greyhen (*bottom left*).
Above and left Sketches of red grouse in the Gardens of the Zoological Society of Scotland.

Pl. 5

Red Grouse. (♂&♀)

Ptarmigan

Ptarmigan

Although restricted to the Highlands of Scotland for the last 150 years, ptarmigan *Lagopus mutus* used to thrive in the Cumbrian mountains particularly during the colder spells of the late 1700s and early 1800s. It is the only resident British bird that moults into an all-white winter plumage whose thick, pure-white feathers provide thermal protection against severe weather as well as camouflage against predators in snow-bound mountains. The mottled grey of the summer plumage blends well with the boulder-strewn slopes and their recumbent lichen growths, so that at a few yards' distance the bird is virtually invisible. In summer it feeds on seeds, shoots and buds, while in the autumn berries form a large part of the diet; in winter it will eat whatever is available.

Though occasionally taken by shooters and poachers, its mountain retreats had seen little of man's influence until the last two decades. The impact of recreation in remote mountain areas and disturbance of breeding and feeding areas by ramblers is a cause for concern to bird conservationists. In the Cairngorms, skiing itself does not seem to have encroached on the ptarmigan's feeding grounds, but damage to the plants and thin soils of the mountains can be heavy and can affect indirectly the summer feeding grounds of other animals.

Left The ptarmigan *Lagopus mutus* in winter (*above*) and autumn plumage (*below*). The bird's colouration changes along with the seasons, providing excellent camouflage on the bare mountain sides against birds of prey, wild cats and men. The white winter feathers are also good protection against the conditions of arctic cold.

Below Ptarmigan Hill, Sutherland. A typical example of the habitat where ptarmigan abound. On these rocky slopes, strewn with lichen-covered boulders, the ptarmigan may be seen feeding on the seeds, berries and shoots of the tundra grasses and shrubs.

Wild Cat

The Caledonian forests in the Highlands remain the last preserve of the fiercest of British mammals, the wild cat *Felis sylvestris*. The past 500 years have seen the decimation of these forests by farmers of cattle, and later sheep, and by wars between the Celtic tribes and British armies. The impact on all the forest faunas has been severe, and without the protection of a handful of land-owning lairds, the wild cat, marten and golden eagle would have disappeared with the sea eagle, wolf and brown bear.

In 1880 the wild cat was found only north of the Great Glen – and then rarely. Ten years later individuals were recorded in Argyllshire and Aberdeenshire, corresponding with widespread re-afforestation programmes. Persecution by gamekeepers seriously depleted all predators, whether bird or mammal, around the grouse moors of the British uplands, but where deer was the sporting animal as in Sutherland and Ross-shire, the eagle and cat were preserved: they controlled mountain hares and birds that would, when flushed by stalkers, frighten the highland stags and spoil the day's sport. But destruction of habitat had taken its toll on the cat. After the First World War, however, extensive forest projects supported by the new Forestry Commission gradually reversed the pattern of Highland agriculture, restoring old haunts for black grouse and capercaillie. Land that had been denuded as rough pasture for cattle and sheep was afforested: wool and mutton from Australia and New Zealand had become cheaper, manpower shortages were considerable after the carnage of war, and financial incentives by governments were some of the economic factors that brought about the change. But the damage to Scottish wildlife had taken its toll by Thorburn's day, and it would have been difficult to have seen in the wild some of the animals he depicted.

The wild cat *Felis sylvestris* is the fiercest of all British animals, although little larger than a big domestic cat. It is now restricted to the undisturbed pine forests of northern Britain. This illustration was based on sketches made of a cat in captivity.

Pl 10
A. Thorburn
1918

The wild cat haunts the shores of lakes, ravines and old forests where it feeds on grouse, mountain hares, small birds and rabbits, although the latter were only introduced to the Highlands in the eighteenth century. When it is cornered in a ravine, or has young, it does not hesitate to attack man, flinging itself at the head, and will put up a good fight against the best hounds. Following the path of re-afforestation, it has spread over the border into the Kielder forest but, because it is nocturnal and wary of human interference, it is rarely seen. Its usefulness for rodent control in new forests, along with the marten and polecat, now ensures its security as a British mammal – a long cry from the virtual extinction of the early years of the twentieth century. Perhaps Cumbria will once again be its haunt after an absence of 250 years.

The feral cat, escaped from man's domesticity, is now widespread through Europe and is easily distinguished from the wild cat by its smaller size and less bushy tail. The lynx *Felis lynx*, a shorter-tailed and larger relative of the cats, still inhabits a few mountain enclaves in Europe. It became extinct in Britain some 3000 years ago when Bronze Age people used it in sorcery. It was present widely in mainland European forests during the last century, disliked by Norwegian and Greek farmers for the sheep and goats it stole, and pursued by the hunter for its valuable fur. Nowadays its future looks as bleak as its Mesolithic remains in Scottish caves.

Pine Marten

Adaptability to changing conditions and habitats assures the survival of many animals in Europe today. Over the last 1000 years, most areas of Britain have been altered to suit man's needs, whether for timber, crops or housing. Fifty years ago it was not in the Scots pines of the Caledonian forest that the pine marten *Martes martes* was found, but across the tree-less moors and hills of western Ross and Sutherland. Though claimed to be extinct in southern England by 1850, martens were present in Devon at the turn of this century, by which time the Lakeland population had retreated to the screes and fell-sides where they fed on voles and small birds.

Many misconceptions about the habits and haunts of the marten were rife in the Victorian literature; these were based on the reports of casual observers. It is clearly an opportunist, like the fox and otter, feeding on the most easily available food, although predominantly a ground-feeder. It is now established that it tends to move to deciduous and open lands in summer from its winter haunts in mixed woodlands. The winter diet of squirrels, voles and birds changes in summer to a rich variety of berries, carrion, eggs and insects. So, the survival of the marten has been ensured by its ability to colonize new habitats and, with re-afforestation projects throughout northern Britain, it has managed to spread and recolonize many of its former regions.

Hunting areas may cover 30 square kilometres, but in mixed mature forest where there is a good supply of prey, these are reduced to 150 hectares. Its territories and social behaviour are still relatively unstudied in Britain but in common with the other members of the weasel family its scent marks the boundary of its range. Also, like the stoat, it mates in late summer although foetal development is only triggered by increasing day length after mid-winter.

An adult pine marten *Martes martes* searching a rotten pine stump for insects. Despite popular belief, martens spend much time searching on the ground for berries, carrion, rodents and eggs, as well as invertebrates. Once common throughout Britain, its main strongholds are the Highlands of Scotland and Ireland.

A. Thorburn. 1919.

Mountain Hare

The Scottish mountain hare *Lepus timidus scotticus* (*left*) and the Irish hare *L. timidus hibernicus* (*right*). Both races are distinguished from the brown hare by their smaller size, shorter ears and absence of black on the top of the tail. The Irish race does not turn white in winter and may be found all over the country.

Its habit of changing colour to white in winter has given the mountain hare the alternative names of the varying hare, blue hare and alpine hare. The Scottish race *Lepus timidus scotticus* has its stronghold in the Highlands of Scotland where it is found over 300 metres along with the other arctic inhabitants, the ptarmigan and snow bunting. The brown hare is not found in Ireland, but the Irish hare, a race of mountain hare *L. timidus hibernicus* occurs in a wide variety of habitats. On mainland Britain, the two hare species are mutually exclusive in their distributions; lowland fields and open woods are not colonized by the mountain hare.

The Irish hare does not change colour in winter. In its native Ireland where the winters are not harsh like those in Scotland, the hare retains its summer russet coloration throughout the year. The changing pelt colour is due to a moult although at one time it was thought to come about through the action of cells absorbing

The mountain hare *Lepus timidus* is also known as the blue, varying and alpine hare because it moults the summer colours for a thick, white pelt as winter approaches and snow falls. This provides camouflage against predators and protection against heat loss.

the fur pigment at low temperatures. Moulting is triggered by the onset of winter and the decreasing temperatures; the colder the climate, the greater the proportion of white fur. So the camouflage is effective at all times against an open and barren landscape where any medium-sized animal is ready prey for eagles, martens and wild cats.

On the remote hills of southern Scotland, the Pennines and Wales, successful introductions were made during the last century. The Border Forest Parks in Northumbria and Cumbria have now become a stronghold of this once rare animal. Like the rabbit and brown hare, three litters a year are not uncommon, and on average a doe produces six to seven young each year following her birth. Unlike the brown hare, the mountain hare excavates a simple burrow in the hillsides during the breeding season, supposedly in preparation for the birth of the young. The leverets may use this burrow as shelter from bad weather and their predators.

Birds of prey

The soaring flight and rapacity of eagles has always captivated man's imagination. The Greeks named the golden eagle *Aquila chrysaetos* 'the bird of heaven' as it soared higher than all other birds. The association with strength and superiority has made it the national emblem of many countries. Fables, myths and legends abound, and the lack of objective study of its habits has led to misjudgments of its true nature and contributed much to its demise. Until the Scottish clearances, the golden eagle was a widespread inhabitant of the Highlands, and the Welsh and Irish uplands. But with the development of deer forests, grouse moors and sheep hills, persecution became rife. In the eyes of landowners and gamekeepers, any predator was a pest. Bounties paid for the white-tailed sea eagle, among other animals, accelerated these destructive forces. There was a general lack of understanding of the inter-relationships between predators and their natural prey, and the balancing control these predators exerted on rodent, hare and bird populations.

Eagles tend to feed on live prey of medium size, catching it while flying close to the ground. Mountain hare and grouse on average make up 50 and 30 per cent of prey weight respectively, but mammals and birds to the size of deer calves and herons are also taken. In winter, carrion is abundant on the hills and mountains, and lamb carrion is a major food source in the bad weather of early spring. The average territory of a pair of eagles with juveniles is in the region of 60 square kilometres. The impact of a breeding pair would not be great therefore on a well-stocked grouse moor. The 100 to 150 grouse taken in a year is minimal compared with the many thousands taken by the gun, and the eagles' toll generally does not include the resident breeding population of grouse. Despite legal protection of birds of prey, some grouse estates still purposely disturb eagles' eyries during the breeding season, or are the 'accidental' cause of eagles being poisoned. Usually attacks on birds of prey are carried out with impunity, as they cannot be proven.

The introduction and widespread use of organochlorine insecticides, Dieldrin, Aldrin and DDT in agriculture have had a considerable effect on birds of prey, and were probably the cause of the marked reduction in golden eagles during the 1950s and 1960s. Aldrin used in sheep-dipping was picked up by eagles feeding on sheep carrion. In common with other pesticides, Aldrin and Dieldrin accumulate in the body of predators and are present in the eggs of contaminated birds, affecting the chicks' chances of survival.

Eagles have since returned to their earlier breeding success with the banning of such chemicals, and their populations are now regarded as steady overall. But outside the western Highlands the eagles are being subjected to ever increasing interference from climbers, birdwatchers and others, and some governmental control of eagle breeding sites is needed to prevent any further retraction of the eagles' haunts.

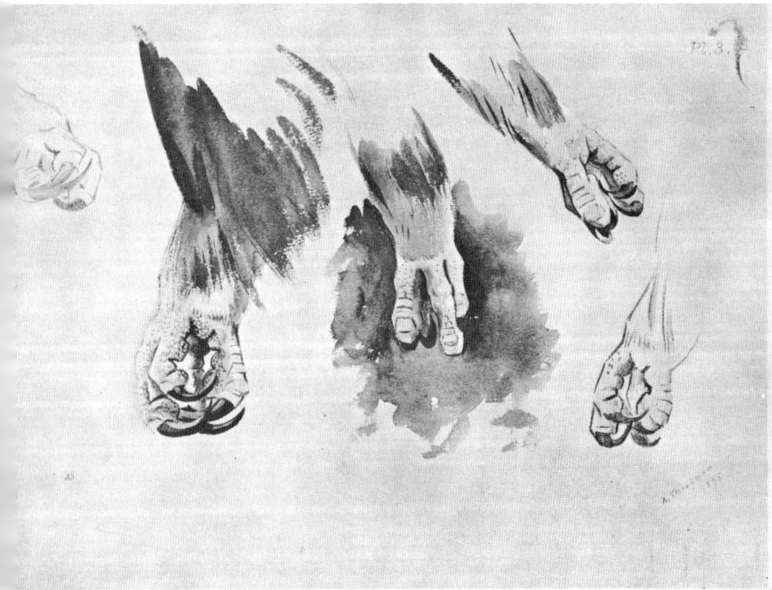

Opposite A winter scene showing a golden eagle *Aquila chrysaetos* with a mountain hare in its grasp. This prey makes up half the average diet of the eagle.
Left Detail of the claws of a golden eagle, showing their adaptation to the killing and lifting of prey. The leg feathers are a characteristic of the eagle.

Pl.

Pl.

Gyr-Falcon *Peregrine Falcon (adult & young)*

Although the form of the head is somewhat stylized in Thorburn's illustrations of the hawks, he has managed to capture the essence of these birds. Historically popular with artists, it is not often that such vitality and life is portrayed in these birds. Thorburn had access to both zoos and private collections where he studied and drew from life, normally a difficulty with wild studies.

In the ancient books of hawking, each nobleman was assigned the type of hawk proper to his rank: a gyrfalcon for a king, a peregrine for an earl, a kestrel for a knave or servant. The importance of falconry was such that the fourth officer in the service of the Celtic Welsh princes was the king's falconer. All birds of prey were strictly protected before the eighteenth century. As the gun became commonly available and accurate, shooting replaced falconry as the provider of sport and game for the table. The protection of the birds of prey quietly disappeared along with many of their woodland haunts. Persecution in the name of gamebird protection made the goshawk and marsh harrier extinct by the end of the last century. Apart from some small respite during the First World War, the numbers of the other raptors were severely depleted by 1939 through persecution by gamekeepers.

The peregrine falcon *Falco peregrinus* is probably the most cosmopolitan of all raptors for it is found in every continent of the world. Eighteen races are known and they live in a wide range of habitats from equatorial desert to sub-arctic forest. In France the peregrine is known as the wandering falcon from its highly migratory and dispersive habits. In the milder maritime climate of Britain it is generally a sedentary resident and rarely disperses more than 80 kilometres from its birthplace.

Like other falcons, the nest is either a simple earth-scrape on an inaccessible cliff ledge or is made in the disused nest of a crow or an eagle. The male peregrine, or tiercel, may help with incubation, and when the eggs hatch provides prey for the female and young. During this period the female becomes aggressive towards any intruder near the nest.

During the war many peregrines were shot to protect military carrier pigeons. In the 1960s, at the request of the racing-pigeon fraternity, the British Trust for Ornithology studied the British falcons, particularly the peregrine, with respect to pigeons. Alarmingly it discovered that the peregrine population was half that before the war and that only a small fraction of this population were raising broods. The decline of the peregrine falcons was reversed with the banning of the persistent organochlorine pesticides Dieldrin and Aldrin in agriculture. Now the peregrine

Opposite An adult male peregrine falcon or tiercel *Falco peregrinus* (*above right*) and a juvenile flying (*above left*). A male gyrfalcon *Falco rusticolus* (*below*) is feeding on a mallard duck.

Above right Detail of an Icelandic gyrfalcon with ruffled feathers, taken on a stormy March day.

is under pressure again with disturbance by climbers and the high prices paid for chicks by falconers.

The Icelandic gyrfalcon *F. rusticolus* was traditionally collected for the kings of northern Europe. It is larger than the peregrine and only breeds in arctic regions, tundra, taiga and coniferous zones, feeding on ptarmigan during winter. Greenland gyrfalcons are regular winter visitors to northern Britain. Recently gyrfalcons have been in demand, especially by Arab falconers, as peregrines become more difficult to acquire. But often it is not realized that the gyrfalcon usually hunts by skimming along the ground rather than by stooping over the prey as the peregrine does, and that it is not tolerant of the middle-eastern climes. To some, survival of the sport seems to be more important than survival of the species.

The kestrel *Falco tinnunculus* is now the commonest raptor, or bird of prey, in Britain. It is most familiar along the verges of motorways where it can be seen hovering in search of its main prey, voles. In Britain it is a dispersive and nomadic bird. In areas with large vole populations, kestrels congregate and rapidly increase in number. This was seen especially in the border hills during the vole plague of 1890 to 1892. Present-day kestrel populations may reach high densities locally: in Richmond Park, for example, the density is six per square kilometre. The kestrel now commonly breeds in parks in town and city centres. Unlike the sparrow hawk *Accipiter nisus*, it does not breed in dense woodlands, preferring scattered woodland patches with open countryside and heaths for hunting. Except in the eastern counties the widespread use of persistent organochlorine insecticides has not seriously affected it as it did other raptors like the peregrine falcon.

Contrary to popular belief, merlins *F. columbarius* hunt small birds of less than 100 grams in weight, mainly larks, pipits and wheatears, and rarely take young gamebirds. Unlike other raptors, the merlin has suffered a steady decline since the 1900s for which no definite explanation can be given: the afforestation of its moorland breeding areas has been minimal and the effect of persistent pesticides on the merlin was probably exaggerated since only when studying pesticides did people notice the failure rate of egg hatching, which can also be affected by poor food and disturbance by man.

The hobby *F. subbuteo*, like the red-footed falcon *F. vespertinus* and the lesser kestrel *F. naumanni*, migrates annually in spring from its African winter grounds to Europe. It breeds chiefly in the southern countries, and is increasing in numbers and distribution in Britain, now the western limit of its range. Both the red-footed falcon and lesser kestrel are summer vagrants; the former is now appearing more often in Britain as it slowly expands its European range.

Man can prevent drastic decreases of falcons with adequate legal protection from his own activities, but cannot stop natural changes in numbers and distribution caused by climate and food.

Above A young merlin *Falco columbarius* in its first plumage showing the jesses and blocks used for training. **Opposite** The long-winged hawks in characteristic poses. Red-footed falcon (*top right*), kestrels (*bottom centre and bottom right*), male hobby (*top left*) and male, female and young merlins (*middle left*).

Pl. 3.

Hobby. ♂.
Merlin (♂, ♀ & young).
Red-footed Falcon. (♂ & ♀)
Lesser Kestrel. ♂.

A. Thorburn
Scops
Hawk Owl.
Tengmalm's Owl (with Dusky Warbler)
Little Owl.

Snowy Owl

Every four years irruptions of the large snowy owl *Nyctea scandiaca* are closely related to the explosion of Norway lemmings. This beautiful owl, twice the size of a barn owl, was an annual visitor to the northern isles during the last century. In 1967 it first bred in Fetlar in the Shetland Isles where it has now become a regular visitor at other times of the year as well, feeding on rabbits and birds. Unlike the other owls, it is predominantly seen in daytime, especially towards dawn and dusk when it is searching the moors for prey. The whitish plumage and yellow eyes of the snowy owl are easy to recognize, though the pale-breasted barn owl is often mistaken for it.

In common with other owls of open country the snowy owl usually makes its nest in a scrape on a hummock of grass on the upland moors, where it lays from four to ten eggs between April and June. The larger female is easily distinguished by the presence of larger black-brown bars on the wings, back and tail, and by its generally greyer appearance.

Opposite The snowy owl *Nyctea scandiaca* is the largest owl seen in Britain, being a winter vagrant on the mainland. The three owls above are hawk, Tengmalm's and scops owls, and all are rare vagrants. The little owl (*middle right*) was introduced to Britain 80 years ago.
Below Two sketches of the snowy owl made in captivity.

Pipistrelle or Common Bat.
Noctule.

Lowland Mammals

The British lowlands were heavily forested 5000 years ago. Now there is hardly anywhere that has not been modified or managed by man. The destruction and fragmentation of woodlands has, in turn, increased and diversified the habitats available to the indigenous wildlife. Most arable fields are relatively barren, but hedges, pasture and common land provide important feeding and breeding sites, comparable with those in woodlands, for the British mammals. Of these, the predators, such as foxes, shrews and weasels, are mainly opportunistic, feeding on the most easily available prey, and may become quite common. The mild winter climate enables herbivorous animals, such as hares and rabbits, to feed and possibly even breed all the year round. The insectivorous bats and hedgehogs circumvent the winter by resting in a state of torpor or hibernation.

Bats

Bats or *Chiroptera* are the second largest order of mammals, being surpassed in number of species only by the rodents. The British species belong to the insectivorous division of the order, the more exotic fruit-eating bats being confined to the tropics. Only three of the thirteen species found in Britain are widely distributed. The rest are restricted in overall distribution, although they may be locally common.

The bats are the only mammals capable of true flight, hence their diagnostic feature, the wing. This consists of a double fold of skin extended over the elongated bones of the fingers and arms. The skin is kept soft by oily secretions, supplied by glands located elsewhere on the body.

The now well known echo-location apparatus of the bat remained a mystery until 1920, when the suggestion was made that bats guided themselves in flight by the emission and subsequent

Pipistrelle *Pipistrellus pipistrellus* (*top left*), and noctule *Nyctalus noctula* (*right and bottom left*). The noctule is a large bat with distinctive dark yellowish-brown fur. It flies high and straight, with frequent swoops presumably for insects. The pipistrelle is the smallest and commonest European bat. Its flight is fast and jerky.

detection of ultrasonic sound. The larynx of the bat, which is responsible for sound production, differs significantly from that of other animals. Additionally the ear is closed by a small muscle when a sound is emitted. This prevents the auditory apparatus from being desensitized and means that it is more capable of detecting the echoed sound.

Since these animals hunt using sound it is not surprising that many insects upon which they prey have evolved countermeasures. One such measure is for the insect to allow itself to fall out of the flight path of the bat simply by folding its wings when bat ultrasounds are detected. This method is employed by the lacewing. The tiger moth, on the other hand, has evolved a means of emitting its own ultrasound which effectively 'scrambles' the bat's echo-location system. This is similar, in principle, to the anti-radar device known as 'window' employed during the last war.

It was probably the principles of radar which inspired the original research upon the ultrasound devices of bats. The strange facial shapes, characteristic of many bats, appear to be an adaptation to enable sound to be directionally emitted.

The technique of high speed filming has shown that many bats do not catch prey using their mouth. Instead, many use the tail membrane or, alternatively, the wing membrane. The prey is then flicked into the mouth and eaten or, in the case of a large insect, devoured on the ground.

The hibernation of bats is well known, as is the predisposition of, for example, the pipistrelle *Pipistrellus pipistrellus* for roosting in belfries. These habits have contributed more to their reduced numbers than any other factor. The bat-proofing of churches has led to a reduction in available habitats in most areas of Britain. Furthermore, the rise in popularity of caving and potholing has meant that species which hibernate in these locations, for example Natterer's bat *Myotis nattereri*, have been subjected to interference, which frequently results in the death of the animal.

Bat researchers themselves have been responsible in the past for depleting numbers by the use of unsuitable 'rings' or 'bonds'. A licence is now required for the tagging of bats. The greater horseshoe bat *Rhinolophus ferrumequinum* is now a protected species in Britain.

Opposite The greater horseshoe bat *Rhinolophus ferrumequinum* (*top*) and the lesser horseshoe bat *Rhinolophus hipposideros* (*below*) are distinguishable from all other bats by the complex lobes of bare skin on the muzzle. **Right** The Natterer's bat *Myotis nattereri* has a characteristic fringe of hairs on the tail membrane.

Red Fox

One of the largest carnivores extant in Britain is the red fox *Vulpes vulpes*. Although hunted as vermin since the Middle Ages by farmers and sportsmen alike, it has managed to survive. It is now seen as much in urban centres as in the depths of rural Britain, and in such widely differing environments as mountains, coastal cliffs and woodland. Part of the success of the fox must be attributed to it being an opportunist, and the fox's present ubiquity is due to this ability to adapt to local conditions and the changes in the environment brought about by man.

Research on the life and habits of foxes has shown that they have varied feeding patterns, habitats and territorial sizes. Their diet consists mainly of small rodents, rabbits and hares as well as invertebrates such as beetles and slugs, and carrion. Much of the fox's persecution has been due to the misconception that it was primarily a predator of livestock.

The increase in accessibility of fox-hunting to the expanding middle classes of the Victorian Age, with their new-found wealth from the Empire, had its effect on fox numbers. At times it became quite scarce. Many thousands were therefore imported and released last century to strengthen ailing local populations. The imported red fox bred with and ousted the long-legged, greyer English variety which now can be found only in the upland areas of the north of England. The development of fox-hunting in the Midlands did, however, promote the preservation of copses and woods for their breeding; where these are still in existence they are now retreats for badgers and wild birds. Occasional respite from the hounds happened with outbreaks of rabies in the hunt kennels, but this disease has not been endemic in the British wild carnivore population for the last 50 years.

Red fox *Vulpes vulpes*. This well known animal is illustrated here in its traditional setting: the beauty of the English hedgerow. Its great adaptability has made it as familiar a sight in urban districts as in the country. In Thorburn's day foxes were mainly seen pursued by the hunt, or adorning the walls of hunting lodges.

Pl. 11
A. Thorburn
1918

Badger

The enthusiasm of man for the extermination of animals which may carry diseases or harm his livestock has recently been strengthened by agriculture becoming seen as a business of economics rather than a peaceful coexistence with nature. The badger *Meles meles* received a severe blow with allegations that it acted as a carrier of bovine tuberculosis, though only laboratory tests have implicated it as transmitter of the disease. There has been widespread shooting, and gassing of setts in southwest England, although protection was brought by the Badger Act of 1974.

Setts are usually in woodland, though thick hedgerows suffice. Often they originate from old foxes' earths or rabbit burrows. The residences can be historic, and very large, rambling old ones with up to a dozen entrances can be found, particularly in Surrey and in southwest England. When disturbed badgers, like moles, readily escape backwards, an ability which facilitates movement along the burrows. Evidence of badgers is the piles of old bedding material and shallow earth scrapings used as latrines and territorial markers. These are mostly scattered at the perimeter of their ranges, with one or two adjacent to the sett. Although nocturnal, when nights are short they may emerge to feed in the late evening, or be seen strolling the boundary of their ranges. In remote areas where man is absent, they sometimes emerge in broad daylight.

In most of Europe the use of badger hair for shaving bristles has been replaced by hog and by synthetic bristles so that their skins no longer have any economic importance, although badger hams are still esteemed as a delicacy.

Contrary to popular thought, badgers do not hibernate. But in severe winters they may enter periods of dormancy when they utilize large subcutaneous fat deposits, rich in the vitamins which are in short supply in winter.

Badgers *Meles meles* use their claws to dig out the nests of wasps. With their flexible and muscular snouts, ideal aids to probing and digging, they can then reach the larvae on which they like to feed. Their thick coats afford them effective protection against the wasps' stings.

The pole cat *Mustela putorius* is often known as the foul marten from its highly offensive smell which it uses in self-defence and in territorial markings. It quickly became scarce in Britain, with the advent of the gamekeepers' traps, but it is now gradually expanding its range around Wales.

The Weasel Group

Polecats *Mustela putorius* are often confused with the feral ferret since both are of similar size, shape and coloration. Crosses between the two animals produce the 'fitch-ferrets' of the hunter, but as with many hybrids these are predominantly sterile. The polecat, wild cat and pine marten have all been heavily persecuted over the last two centuries as vermin and predators of gamebirds, wildfowl and poultry. Even now polecats are sometimes caught in the steel traps and snares laid for squirrel, mink and rat and, along with road-traffic casualties, these account for an estimated 90 per cent of all deaths; the remaining ten per cent are lost by hunting, shooting and dogs. At the turn of this century, the polecat was one of the rarest of the British mammals, but it could still be found in Oxfordshire, Exmoor, Dartmoor, Scotland, Wales and Cumbria. But it was no longer in the outskirts of London where it has been up until 1860. By

The weasel *Mustela nivalis* is the smallest of all the weasel family in Britain, but does not occur in Ireland. Despite its small size, up to 20 cm body length, it will prey on small rabbits and hares, sometimes hunting in family groups like hounds. Minivers are in fact overwintering young weasels.

1940 its distribution had been reduced to Wales and Hertfordshire. Its numbers are now gradually increasing and it is spreading through the English–Welsh border counties. Reports of sightings in other parts of Britain are difficult to substantiate because there are possible confusions with the similar feral ferret. Despite the destruction of the upland woodlands and the disappearance of the wild cat and pine marten, the polecat, or foul marten as it was also known, was equally at home in the rough pastureland of the hills. It was here that the polecat survived and from this stronghold that it has been able to recolonize the large areas of trees and woodlands planted since the last war.

It is unusual for a closely related group of animals to have the diversity of breeding habits exhibited by the weasel group. All mate and have one litter per year except the smallest, the weasel *M. nivalis*, which may produce both a spring and an autumn litter. The stoat *M. erminea* mates in late summer but the partially developed fertilized

In cold climates the stoat *Mustela erminea* generally becomes white in winter, except for the tail tip, to produce the famous ermine fur. On high mountains the ermine may remain white all year. In southern England the stoat may retain its summer colouration completely during the winter, depending on the severity of the weather.

eggs, or blastocysts, remain dormant in the uterus until spring when implantation occurs. Foetal development lasts three to four weeks and a litter of between six and twelve kittens is then produced. On the other hand, the polecat mates during a spring oestrus and foetal development immediately follows, with no delayed implantation of the eggs. The mink has features of both methods. It courts in spring and has a variable delay of blastocyst implantation such that gestation may be anywhere from six to eleven weeks, in contrast to the polecat's six weeks. The litter size of mink and polecats varies from five to ten, and both breed in the year following birth with an estimated life expectancy in the wild of three to five years outside the nest. The stoat is unusual. It is possible for a female to mate at five weeks old with older males and produce a litter the following year. Life expectancy is shorter, at twelve to eighteen months after weaning. The

little weasel lives only a year.

The 'miniver' was thought to be a separate species of weasel for many years because, at only eight to ten centimetres long, it is about half the size of a normal weasel. Now it is realized that minivers are the autumn young which remain juvenile in size during the winter and probably grow to adulthood the following spring. In Europe they were given species status in 1968 as *Mustela minuta*. Their taxonomic status is still debatable.

Stoats are sociable and have been observed hunting in family packs in daylight. The others tend to be territorial and individuals live singly outside the breeding seasons, marking their areas with characteristic putrid-smelling scents. Since they all hunt at night, they have highly developed senses of smell and hearing, but daytime activity is common, and the period of activity tends to be dependent on the activity of their prey.

Common Shrew.

Lesser Shrew

Water Shrew

3

Shrews

The smallest of our British mammals is the pygmy shrew *Sorex minutus*. It occurs throughout the British mainland alongside the common shrew *S. araneus* and the water shrew *Neomys fodiens*. The pygmy shrew is present in the outer Scottish islands with the exception of Shetland and in Ireland where it is the only resident shrew. But being of a retiring habit and of small size it is rarely noticed, whereas its larger relative, the common shrew, is often seen lying dead by wayside paths in autumn. Both these shrews occur in a wide variety of habitats, especially where there is scrub, hedgerows, thick grass or open woodland, although within these areas their niches are different. Competition between them is minimized because the pygmy shrew feeds on smaller invertebrate food and spends more time above the ground than the common shrew. It tends to utilize surface runs of voles, while the common shrew is a more avid burrower in both soil and litter. Earthworms and slugs are important in their diets, but in common with the majority of widespread animals they are quite catholic in their tastes, having preferences as the seasons and food supplies change.

With the increase of long grass and scrub in many areas previously grazed and kept short by rabbits, new habitats for shrews are becoming available. In turn, shrews could be one of the factors in the demise of our scarcer insects such as the chalk-hill and adonis blue butterflies, as they are rapacious creatures with never-ending appetites. The smaller the body, the larger the surface area in relation to its volume, and the greater the loss of heat. To compensate for this, shrews must feed 24 hours a day, with only the occasional couple of hours rest. They must also keep this up both in winter and summer. Even a day's starvation causes inevitable death. In turn, they are both an important food source for the barn owl and to a lesser extent the tawny owl. But fox and cat rarely eat them although they are often caught. It may be that, in common with man who eats only the flesh of herbivores, cats and dogs find that shrew flesh is bitter. This helped perhaps to encourage the folklore and old myths that have arisen around 'those dark and evil shrewmice'.

Absent from Ireland, the larger water shrew is most often encountered around the herbaceous margins of clean-water pools and streams, especially in the watercress beds of southern England, jumping into the water at the slightest hint of danger, but still easy prey for the ever hungry mink and pike. Despite its adaptation to a watery habitat, it is sometimes discovered in coniferous and broadleaved woodlands a few kilometres away from water.

There do not seem to be any significant changes in shrew distributions since Thorburn's day. But as is the case with many smaller creatures, the shrew elicited little interest from the early Victorians whose studies usually concerned of stuffed trophies for decoration, or preservation for sport and hunting. The artists of Thorburn's era helped enormously to change these attitudes by depicting the wide range of fauna and flora which all have important parts to play in the heritage of Britain.

Opposite The common shrew *Sorex araneus* (*top left*), the water shrew *Neomys fodiens* (*bottom*), and the smallest British mammal the pygmy shrew *S. minutus* (*top right*). All three are insectivorous.
Right The tawny owl *Strix aluco* in its daytime roost.

Hedgehog

At the onset of winter the hedgehog, dormouse and bat are all capable of hibernating. They find a suitable retreat and switch off most bodily functions. The only indications of life are the merest whisper of a depressed heart beat and slow respiration, while the body temperature falls to near the ambient. With the onset of spring the hedgehog *Erinaceus europaeus* becomes a regular visitor to hedgerows and gardens at night time. It is found throughout Britain to the tree-line, but is generally scarce in coniferous woods, marshes and moorlands. It requires grassland close to its woodland, scrub or hedgerow retreats, where it wanders from dusk to dawn searching for worms, insects, frogs, young birds and eggs. It has been presumed to eat gamebird eggs, although overall such damage is minute, and instances of its attacking birds and young rabbits have been thought improbable. But, as if in support of this theory, a single individual of the related Mediterranean species was known to have opened a door propped shut against feral cats and killed 12 six-week-old pullets in three nights before it was destroyed. Generally the British hedgehog is liked by the gardener for its usefulness in eating slugs and snails in gardens and orchards.

Evidence of hedgehogs is all too frequently witnessed by the numbers killed on the roads at night. Their instinctive reflex of curling up into a ball is no defence in this man-made situation. But when curled up predation by foxes and cats is hindered, though young and sickly individuals are readily taken by stoat, fox and polecat. Stone Age man of Mesolithic times ate hedgehogs, and in parts of Europe they are still said to be eaten by gipsies who cook them in clay. Hedgehogs have been implicated as carriers of foot-and-mouth disease and contagious abortion-fever in cattle. Another legend, that of their suckling cow's udders for milk, has yet to be substantiated.

The hedgehog *Erinaceus europaeus* is the most commonly seen British insectivore. The characteristic tough spines are closely set on its back, the underside of its face and legs being covered with hair.

Mole

In common with other insectivorous mammals, the mole *Talpa europaea* feeds on live animal food, usually worms, beetles and slugs. It is rarely seen above ground although it is sometimes presented by cats to their unappreciative owners. The familiar molehills formed during the excavation of burrows makes it a scourge of lawns and farmland. The front legs are powerful and well adapted for digging and it can run equally well backwards as forwards. Its soft, velvety fur can be brushed both ways, another adaptation for burrowing.

Worms migrate through the soil according to season; the moles burrow correspondingly at different depths. In frost and drought the tunnels are deep, while in summer feeding is in the shallow runs and at the surface where frogs and insects also may be taken. In poorer soils containing fewer worms, the burrows and molehills are more extensive than in soils of richer yield. Burrow systems in undisturbed areas are often generations old, but only one mole will occupy a single territory at a particular time. However territories are not as rigid temporally and spatially as they are with otters and wild cats.

Moles pair in February and March, the only time that adults meet without fighting. At other times of the year moles will attack each other with great ferocity. In April and May the young are born in a nest lined with dry grass and leaves, and they grow to adult size in about three weeks.

The Victorian molecatcher with his willow switch has been replaced by modern break-back traps so the persecution by farmers continues. The main enemy, however, is changing methods of farming using deep ploughing, and the removal of hedgerows. Slit seeding and 'chemical ploughing' with paraquat probably have little effect since the land is less disturbed here than it is in the moles' traditional habitats.

Like shrews, moles feed throughout the day and night, though the 24-hour day is organized into roughly three rest and three active periods during which there is a constant check on the state of the tunnels, feeding from each in rotation. Often one of the runs will lead to the edge of a dyke or stream from which the mole can drink. They have been known to cross a few hundred metres of water to reach islands, or just to swim for no apparent reason; their forelegs being as well designed for paddling as for burrowing. How they locate an island with such limited eyesight is not known, and their tendency to take the shortest route is still a puzzle.

The mole *Talpa europaea*. Totally adapted to an underground existence, its strong fossorial forepaws enable it to dig at an amazing pace. Although rarely noticed above ground, it both runs and swims with equal ease, crossing roads or streams with assurance. Its food is predominantly worms, grubs and beetles.

A.Thorburn
1918

Squirrels

Did the American grey squirrel *Sciurus carolinensis* drive the red squirrel *S. vulgaris* out of England? The coincidence of the expansion of the grey and the corresponding decline of the red has led to a general acceptance of this theory, but three factors appear to have influenced the red's decline: epidemics of disease, the harsh winters at the beginning of the 1800s and trapping for fur. Man's fragmentation and destruction of their native coniferous and mixed woodland, both in England and Wales, for agriculture and building, resulted in local extinctions. The end of the nineteenth century saw large areas of Scotland under reafforestation with Scots pine and introduced conifers, and it was then that the red squirrel started to increase its numbers.

Between 1830 and 1920 both more reds from Europe and the American grey were introduced into up to 30 areas in England, and the lowlands of Scotland and Ireland. The ecological vacuum left by the local red squirrel extinctions allowed colonization by the grey in the woodlands and hedgerows of southern England. The extent of this colonization is at present over eleven million hectares. The grey's tolerance of human presence has made it a common sight in city centres and suburbia where it is regarded as an asset. Meanwhile the red, although expanding its range, is restricted to more undisturbed areas of the quiet northern forests.

Normally the grey squirrel is a quiet and harmless animal and is of no economic importance. In the relatively predator-free environment of England, grey squirrels will breed twice a year. Numbers consequently build up to high densities. If there is no room for juveniles to claim their own territories, they congregate in bands and behave like human juvenile vandals, damaging and destroying trees.

Red squirrel *Sciurus vulgaris*. Passing the greater part of its life among the branches of trees, the strong flexible feet and sharp claws enable it to maintain a hold on boughs with the greatest ease. The long, bushy tail acts both as a balance in climbing and as protection against cold.

Pl.24
A. Thorburn
1919.

Pl.3

Field-Vole.

Bank Vole.

3

In Scotland there appears to have been a separate and darker race of the red squirrel living in pine forests and feeding predominantly on pine seeds. Thorburn illustrated this form of the red squirrel which has, during the last decade, expanded into the Border forests of the Pennines along with the pine marten, its major arboreal predator in Britain. But in winter, both species of squirrel spend more time on the ground, where they feed on nuts, berries and fungi, and where they are frequently taken by cats, stoats, foxes and birds of prey. Now the greatest potential predator is man with his ability to destroy or change their woodland haunts.

Voles

The tremendous population explosion of the field vole *Microtus agrestis* in 1891 to 1894 had a serious effect on the sheep and cattle farmers of Northumberland and the Scottish lowlands. Within weeks large areas of their grazing lands had been destroyed and many a livelihood ruined. Turkey was experiencing a vole plague at the same time. The British Government therefore sent a commission to investigate and learn any measures that the Turks had discovered to combat their plague. In 1893, when the British plague was abating, the reply from the great Ottoman Empire came: '. . . and with the Holy water procured from Mecca, a few drops are sprinkled on to the affected fields with a prayer. The rest is trusted to God. . . .'

In the north the solution was natural: after the boom came the crash. The vole has an inbuilt mechanism that is dependent on population density. As numbers increase, the voles become aggressive and their reproduction rate rapidly decreases because the animals attack one another and cease to breed, while ill-health and death increase. Vole populations naturally fluctuate in three- to four-year cycles. A series of optimal conditions, such as mild winters and few predators, occasionally coincide, allowing this highly fecund animal to multiply like greenfly on a rose bush. Two other vole plagues are recorded: one in the Scottish lowlands in 1874 to 1876 and another in 1580 in Essex when a plague of short-eared owls was also noticed. Toward the summer of 1892, many of these owls were seen in the vole-stricken north along with foxes, barn owls, stoats and kestrels, all important predators of the vole. With abundant supplies of their food available, numbers of predators had also increased greatly, but their impact on the established plague was minimal. Now it is realized that the breeding success of the kestrel and barn owl are dependent on the abundance of these small rodents, and that predation is necessary to prevent the voles reaching the critical density from which a plague may escalate. Since myxomatosis and the demise of the rabbit, foxes, stoats and birds of prey have increased the proportion of voles in their diets.

The bank vole *Clethrionomys glareolus* is redder than the greyish-brown field vole, but demonstrates the vole shape with the shortened head and tail, small eyes and ears, and longish pelt. It is more frequently a resident of the hedgerows, woods and thick cover than of the undisturbed pasture and grasslands of the field vole. Its diet is more diverse, supplementing the grasses of the other voles with fruits, seeds, nuts and leaves. In thick cover the tawny owl, the stoat and the weasel are its main enemies.

In the past, many races and new species of voles and mice have been described from the islands around the British mainland. Nowadays most taxonomic studies are made with reference to the European and Asian faunas and a new understanding of these island races is now possible. It was thought that the island voles of Orkney and Guernsey might be of Iberian origin, having evolved into island races after their introduction by Bronze Age seafarers some 3000 years ago. But remains pre-dating this have been discovered in the Orkney caves, proving that these island voles are a race of the common vole *Microtus arvalis* of Europe.

The bank vole *Clethrionomys glareolus* (*top*), field vole *Microtus agrestis* (*left*) and Orkney vole *M. arvalis*. Compared with the mice, the distinctive character of voles lies in their short, rounded heads, small eyes, short ears and tails, and a general stoutness of form.

Mice

The numbers of Britain's smallest rodent the harvest mouse *Micromys minutus* are said to have declined extensively since the introduction of close-cutting machines. Tall herbage of weed and reeds provide the natural haunt of this mouse, and it once thrived in the perfect habitat offered by man's cereal crops. In Gilbert White's day the characteristic woven nests, the size of a cricket ball, used commonly to be found attached to the stalks of wheat or among the stooks of wheat sheaves in winter. But the changing ways of agriculture have taken their toll. In the wetlands of East Anglia, harvest mice can be found nesting among the reedbeds using reeds and rushes in place of the wheatgrass of the farmlands. But present records do indicate that the harvest mouse is becoming more common and widespread than it was thirty years ago. Is it the decreasing use of pesticides or is it that current observers are more diligent in their searches?

The yellow-necked mouse *Apodemus flavicollis* was not recognized in Britain until the naturalist De Winton described it in 1894. Consequently, little is known about it historically, although numbers do not appear to have fluctuated over the last 80 years. At first sight it is similar to the wood mouse *Apodemus sylvaticus*, perhaps a little heavier, but the large yellow band running across the chest and the richer chestnut red of the pelt confirms the yellow-necked diagnosis. Its habitats are similar to those of the wood mouse, in woodlands, gardens and hedgerows, and both mice climb readily where they feed on seeds, nuts and buds and also on insects. The discarded flesh of fruits and berries is often a reminder of the nocturnal activities of these small mammals.

The yellow-necked mouse *Apodemus flavicollis* (*above*) was not recognized in Britain until 1894. The yellow band on the chest easily distinguished it from the wood mouse *A. sylvaticus* (*opposite below*), a duller and greyer species. The harvest mouse *Micromys minutus* (*opposite above*) is the smallest British mouse, once common in cereal crop fields, where it nested and, with its prehensile tail, easily moved among the corn stems.

Harvest Mouse.

A. Thorburn
1919

Rabbit

The absence of an Anglo-Saxon or old Celtic name for the ubiquitous rabbit *Oryctolagus cuniculus* is evidence for its recent introduction to the British Isles. 'Rabbit' derives from the Norman French 'rabbette', a young rabbit, and the American 'coney' from the Old French for an adult rabbit. Never abundant in the dry, sparse habitats of its native Iberia and southern Europe, it thrived in the rich and lush lands of western Europe. Like the roe deer and the pheasant, the rabbit was established by the Normans in their parkland enclosures, especially in the large turf-walled warrens of the Brecklands and the Downs. During the Middle Ages they were an important source of meat and fur, but neglect during the Civil War in the seventeenth century saw this culture die out. By the 1700s, introductions to other parts of Britain and subsequent escapes had established the rabbit as a widespread inhabitant of the British Isles. Its impact on the countryside was not significant, however, until the beginning of the nineteenth century. Then numbers increased, constantly helped by widespread clearances of broadleaved woodlands and introductions of grazing lands. By the 1930s the number of rabbits was estimated at 50 millions, and 20 years later at nearly 100 millions. Constant cropping by rabbits prevented the land reverting to scrub and eventually woodland, thus creating the acres of short grassland characteristic of the Downs and certain coastlands. In some areas burrowing caused erosion on thin upland soils, but this disturbed soil has provided important food sources for many seed-eating birds.

Control by predators has never been successful although rabbits provide an easy meal for foxes, stoats and many birds of prey, particularly in times of food shortages. Rabbits made up one half of foxes' total consumption. But by 1950 agricultural production was becoming seriously depressed; rabbits were over-grazing winter cereal crops and sheep and cattle pastures.

The tables were turned when, in 1954 and 1955, the deadly rabbit virus myxomatosis was introduced to Britain. This virus is transmitted in the nest by the rabbit flea, and warrens all over the country were decimated within months. Agricultural production started to rise but many predators lost their major food source and turned to rats, voles and birds. The proportion of rabbit in foxes' diets declined to one tenth of the intake, with the corresponding rise in voles from 10 to 40 per cent. Complete elimination of the rabbit never occurred. Some animals survived, and there was selection against living in warrens, where the rabbit flea thrived, towards a solitary hedgerow existence. Consequently rabbit populations occasionally resurge but are kept in check by the now endemic disease.

The effects of this virus are visible on the British landscape. The remnants of old common land are reverting to scrub, oak and beech woodlands with new habitats appearing for woodland birds and mammals. Such succession is, of course, at the expense of the open grassland fauna.

The rabbit *Oryctolagus cuniculus* thrives on light, sandy soils with plenty of cover, but sometimes inhabits almost any ground not too exposed or damp. When travelling to and fro, it keeps to favourite tracks or runs through the grass and herbage. This habit is well known to rabbit catchers who set their snares accordingly.

Brown Hare

One mammal which is commonly seen on British farmland is the hare *Lepus capensis*. Larger and longer-legged than the rabbit, the hare is an animal of the open country where it occurs up to 2000 feet in England, Wales and Ireland and to 1000 feet in Scotland. Fluctuations in numbers occur without apparent cause.

Historically important as a game animal, early English laws protected the hare as an animal of the chase, but over-hunting last century so diminished numbers that individuals were seen only in some of the parks of eastern England. Hares are now associated with flat farmland and are rarely found more than a kilometre away. Its status as a pest is unsure: its food source is predominantly bark, straw and hard vegetation, rather than the grass of the rabbit, and it probably only damages crops in severe food shortages.

Foxes are the main predators on the young hares or leverets which, although well camouflaged, are exposed above ground from the moment of birth. Modern machinery, too, kills many as they lie in their open forms, and this may explain the decline of the hare in some parts of the Midlands.

The sight of groups of hares on grey winter days is indicative of their gregarious habits from autumn to spring. At the onset of March, the breeding males begin their strange and beautiful courtship displays: mock fights and boxing matches are enacted to attract females.

The brown hare *Lepus capensis* produces two to five young at a time. February and March are the usual courting months, and the bucks fight savagely for the does. It can be distinguished from the mountain hare by its long ears, brighter yellow-brown colour and dark upper surface of the tail.

Pl.
Mealy Redpoll.
Serin.
Lesser Redpoll.
Citril Finch.
Linnet
Brambling (Summer & winter)
Tree Sparrow.

Lowland and Woodland Birds

The British lowlands and woodlands provide a great variety of habitats, which have largely been added to by man's activities. The older hedgerows were originally the borders of woods which were felled to provide land for agriculture. These hedgerows still have a diverse flora and fauna like that associated with old woodlands. With the formation of enclosures from the early eighteenth century onwards, many more hedgerows were planted, especially hawthorn. Until recently, these narrow strips of bushes provided a stable habitat for a rich and diverse wildlife. The present changes in agricultural techniques often result in widespread hedgerow clearance that gives the new prairie-type fields a barren and desolate appearance. Not only do birds which nest in the hedgerows, such as chaffinches and dunnocks, disappear, but predatory and parasitic insects are also removed when hedgerows are cut down: insects which would otherwise help in controlling agricultural pests and weeds.

Between 1933 and 1961 no less than 8000 square kilometres of common land, heathland and moors were lost, and there was a 50 per cent rise, to 18,500 square kilometres, in the amount of urbanized land. Roads accounted for 2000 square kilometres of which a third consisted of grass verges. The grassland of the motorway verges now provides admirable breeding ground for voles and mice. These in turn supply the needs of the lowland birds of prey such as kestrels and owls. In addition, the plant and insect life of this steppe-type environment attracts skylarks.

The woodland birds may be divided into four main groups. Firstly, there are those which nest in the woods but feed largely in the surrounding countryside: the canopy-nesting woodpigeons and rooks. Secondly, there are the tree- and shrub-feeding species: the tits, woodpeckers and most of the migrants. Thirdly, there are the thrushes, blackbirds and wrens which are found feeding on the lower levels, on the ground or among low herbage. Finally come the predatory birds: the short-winged hawks and the owls.

The broadleaved woodland canopy contains a few resident species. Woodpigeons and rooks are the most noticeable inhabitants, making their untidy nests among the upper branches. Some tits and small insectivorous songbirds feed in this layer, but not the pigeons and rooks. They move to the surrounding countryside to feed during the day, and return to roost in the evening. In autumn and winter, acorns and beechmast may be taken from the woodland floor by woodpigeons.

Opposite The finches, Fringillidae, are drawn together with the tree and house sparrows. In the breeding season the young are fed mainly on insects; the rest of the year they are predominantly seed eaters.

Right The great tit or ox-eye *Parus major*, easily distinguished from the other tits by its large size and black colouring on the underside and throat.

Pigeons and Doves

The widespread destruction of the woodpigeon's predators along with a nationwide increase in woodlands since the last century both helped to foster the woodpigeon's expansion in numbers and range. Thus the huge flocks, whose numbers are bolstered with winter migrants from Europe, became the farmers' blight of the 1950s and 1960s, ravaging large areas of winter cereals and vegetable crops. Although many thousands of these birds were shot and poisoned, it was natural mortality in the severe winters that actually controlled their numbers. Meanwhile the poison campaigns led to the deaths of many other animals which ate either the treated baits or the dead and dying pigeons. The decline of predators such as foxes, owls and crows allowed their prey animals to increase in numbers and as a consequence there were problems with voles and insects in some localities in the following years. When man indirectly or directly disturbs the precarious balance of nature, unforeseen problems arise elsewhere. This will continue to happen until we gain a better understanding of the inter-relationships of predators and prey, plants and herbivores.

The grey hordes of feral pigeons in city centres and flocks of woodpigeons in fields are a familiar sight these days. Pigeons must rank equally with sparrows and starlings as colonizers of the man-made habitats of this century. Since Thorburn's day the Asiatic collared dove *Streptopelia decaocto* has naturally joined the British and European lists. Although also a seed-eating bird, it has found its niche without directly competing with the other four species of pigeons, the stock dove, the woodpigeon, the turtle dove and the rock dove. The stock dove *Columba oenas* is a bird of open parklands and nests in old tree-hollows, cliffs, ruins and sometimes rabbit holes, The woodpigeon *Columba palumbus* nests in trees and large bushes and feeds mainly in agricultural land. The turtle dove *Streptopelia turtur* breeds in thickets and hedges of the lowlands and valleys and takes weed seeds as its main food source, whilst the rock dove *Columba livia*, ancestor of domesticated and feral pigeons, is still found on coastal cliffs of Ireland and western Scotland.

The start of the spectacular spread of the collared dove was first noted when it had reached the Ottoman Empire in the sixteenth century. By the 1800s it had reached eastern Europe. Its colonization of Europe at an ever increasing rate is due, some claim, to the decline of domesticated doves. Immigrants from France continued this westward trend to England in the 1950s and by 1969 breeding had been recorded in all English counties. All but a few Scottish islands had become regular haunts of the collared dove by the mid-1960s. But there is still no full explanation for this spread, although theories of a genetic change from the original Asiatic stock are being investigated.

The pigeons, Columbidae, are mainly seed-eaters. Their explosive expansion in Britain over the last 50 years rivals that of the fulmar and kittiwake. Each species is depicted in its characteristic habitat. Pallas's sand grouse *Syrrhaptes paradoxus* (*below*) is a rare irregular vagrant to Britain.

Wood Pigeon Stock Dove.
Turtle Dove. Pallas's Sand-Grouse. (♂ & ♀) Rock Dove.

Carrion Crow. Rook. Hooded Crow.

Crows

The wings of crows and jackdaws were placed on the funeral pyres of Scandinavian Bronze Age kings. The belief was that these wings then carried the soul of the king safely up to the heavens and returned it for its rebirth on earth. Members of the crow family continued to play a part in folklore and customs throughout Europe: ravens were the portenders of evil, rooks of success, and in Norway nesting magpies protected houses from ill-fortune and sickness. There are many versions of the magpie verse:

> One for sorrow, two for mirth,
> Three a wedding, four a birth.
> Five for silver, six for gold,
> Seven for a secret ne'er to be told.
> Eight for Heaven, nine for Hell
> And ten for the devil's ain sell.

All corvids in Britain have suffered at the hands of gamekeepers and farmers at one time or another, and by the end of the nineteenth century had reached very low numbers and, in some areas, extinction. But unlike some of the birds of prey, total extinction never occurred in Britain, and we have still the same carrion and hooded crows, *Corvus corone*, magpies *Pica pica*, rooks *C. frugilegus*, ravens *C. corax*, jackdaws *C. monedula* and choughs *Pyrrhocorax pyrrhocorax* that were present in Stone Age Britain 4000 years ago.

The First World War saw an important period of respite for much of our wildlife. The cessation of gamekeeping during this period was followed by a dramatic increase in numbers of crows and rooks in our southern counties. Many of their former haunts were recolonized. Heavy trapping in the post-war period reduced their numbers again, but a decline in the importance of grouse moors has helped to increase the populations of these birds.

The rook *Corvus frugilegus* (*top*), hooded crow *C. corone cornix* (*right*) and carrion crow *C. corone corone* (*left*) are partial migrants that return to their nesting sites in late winter from the coastal and lowland feeding grounds. Many of the large rookeries are of ancient origin, and are used every year.

The effect of hooded crows on gamebirds can be severe during the breeding season with eggs and young birds suffering heavy mortality. Sometimes poachers were regarded as worse enemies by the gamekeeper, but a poor crofter taking a few grouse to supplement a meagre diet was nothing compared to the ravages of a pair of crows feeding an ever-hungry brood. Poisoned baits are used on estates to control crows, since the banning of steel traps, though other forms of wildlife, including golden eagles, buzzards, stoats and polecats are also killed by these poisons.

The carrion crow is the same species as the hooded crow, but whereas the hooded crow breeds in Scotland and Ireland, the carrion crow breeds on the British mainland south of the Great Glen. Interbreeding occurs where these subspecies overlap, and intermediate colour forms may be found. The carrion crow is now associated with urban developments, scavenging at waste tips and in gardens. Alongside roads it is commonly seen with rooks, magpies and jackdaws feeding on dead birds and mammals killed by motor traffic.

The rookery is a characteristic sight of the British countryside. These communal nesting sites at the tops of tall trees in copses and woodland edges are normally within the vicinity of arable land. Some date back many centuries and may contain several hundred nests.

The rook is a partial migrant, like the hooded and carrion crows, and returns in late winter from its coastal feeding grounds to rehabilitate the nests in preparation for egg-laying in early March. Young birds and eggs of other species make up a large proportion of the rook's food at this time, especially when each pair is raising four or five large fledglings. Their damage to cereal, potato and root crops has annoyed farmers since the Middle Ages, but their usefulness in eradicating many insect pests of arable and pasture land probably outweighs this. The loss of many elms stricken by Dutch elm disease will undoubtedly affect rooks and kestrels. 60 per cent of nests in Oxfordshire were in elm copses; and in Huntingdonshire elms are often the only trees. Already the number of nests per square kilometre in Oxfordshire has declined from fifteen in 1944 to nine in 1975; the decrease nationally over the same period was 43.5 per cent.

Kites, ravens and carrion crows played an important part in the processing and removal of edible waste matter from cities and towns in the Middle Ages. This role was recognized, and many edicts and laws were published to secure their protection. The carrion crow and raven still play an important part in removing natural carrion. Along with wolves, ravens followed Napoleon's marches across Europe, feeding on the human carrion of the battlefields. The last 50 years have seen the raven increase but it is still quite rare, and is restricted to upland areas and to coastal cliffs.

The magpie was absent from Ireland up until at least 1670, but the exact date of its introduction is unknown. In Britain, the magpie was abundant during the seventeenth century, but by the early nineteenth century it was quite a rare bird, probably because of the destruction of tall hedgerows and woods. More recently it has

Opposite The magpie *Pica pica* (*left*) and jackdaw *Corvus monedula* (*right*) have recently become more common because of decreased persecution. The raven *Corvus corax* (*bottom*) is shown feeding on a ptarmigan, its normal prey in the Highlands.
Below Studies on a raven feeding and cawing.

Magpie. Raven. Jackdaw.

Pl.
A. Thorburn 1913
Starling. (Summer & winter)
Rose-coloured Starling. (adult & young)
Nutcracker

achieved a gradual expansion from the north and west into the southern and eastern counties where persecution by keepers had at one time been greater.

The nutcracker *Nucifraga caryocatactes* is a rare winter vagrant to coniferous and hazel woodlands being seen mostly in south and east England. This crow takes its name from its fondness for walnuts in France, a trait shared by the rook. Usually the birds recorded come from southern Scandinavia, but in 1968 a large number that arrived were of Siberian origin. This was the result of a sudden increase in the Siberian population, which then spread over western Europe.

The most woodland-dwelling and colourful of the crow family is the jay *Garrulus glandarius*. It is always associated with trees, being seen in hedges, parks, orchards and gardens, beside its normal broadleaved-woodland haunts. If not gregarious, it can be called highly social. When the raucous shriek of a jay is heard, another will reply in the neighbourhood. Various specific alarm calls have been noted when intruders are present. Different alarms are used for stoats, squirrels, kestrels and man. Fledglings and eggs of other birds are sometimes taken by jays, and consequently the jay has earned a bad reputation from the gamekeeper in the past. This and its beautiful plumage led it to be heavily persecuted in the last century. Since the 1920s it has recovered its numbers and range throughout Britain, and now breeds in every county up to the Scottish lowlands, and from the Clyde north to the central Highlands.

Its diet is quite varied, like that of the other crows. Small rodents, insects, berries and slugs are eaten when available. In autumn acorns and beechmast become major food sources, and regeneration of oaks is aided by jays burying acorns, as squirrels do, and then forgetting them. Gardens often suffer from jays raiding them for soft fruits and peas.

Both jays and starlings *Sturnus vulgaris* use ants in the care of their feathers. The jays allow the ants to crawl over their feathers whilst starlings actively rub them in with their beaks. The function of this_behaviour seems to be the control of parasitic mites, the formic acid which the ants discharge acting as an inseciticde. 'Anting' is confined, as far as is known, to the passerine or songbirds.

British starlings are joined in winter by many immigrants from western Europe. Flocks of this gregarious bird may number millions, causing severe damage and fouling in the night-time roosts. Cities and towns are frequently used for roosting, the birds foraging in surrounding countryside and gardens during the day. On the continent the starlings are greatly appreciated by farmers as they feed on leatherjackets and wireworms, important pests of pasture and grasslands. But in England they are disliked for their habit of breeding in house eaves and for their noisiness.

The starling *Sturnus vulgaris* (*top left*), the rosy starling *S. roseus* (*top right*), the chough *Pyrrhocorax pyrrhocorax* (*bottom right*), the jay *Garrulus glandarius* (*bottom left*) and the nutcracker *Nucifraga caryocatactes* (*middle left*). The chough is a costal crow and the rosey starling a rare vagrant. **Right** A starling singing, when the wings are shaken rapidly and the feathers puffed out.

Woodpeckers

The woodpeckers are a specialized group of woodland birds adapted to feeding on insects under the bark and inside the wood of trees. Three species are resident breeders in Britain, the green woodpecker *Picus viridis*, the lesser spotted woodpecker *Dendrocopos minor* and the greater spotted woodpecker *D. major*. Although all three are associated with broadleaved woodlands, the greater spotted woodpecker is equally at home in coniferous woods, and is now the most common and widespread woodpecker in Britain. A hundred years ago this bird had become extinct in Scotland and northern England but it has now recolonized these areas. The green woodpecker is the largest of the three and is found in well-timbered parks, gardens, farmland and woodlands. It is readily noticed for it often feeds on the ground, searching for ants. The lesser spotted woodpecker is about the size of a sparrow, and occasionally leaves woods to feed on soft fruits in the garden.

All these species bore into trees, both for searching out insect grubs and making nestholes. Larvae of wood-boring beetles, moths and wood-wasps are located in their tunnels when the bird drills its hole, and then extracted by the extremely long, dexterous, barb-tipped tongue. Woodpeckers are capable of greatly extending the tongue as they have a curiously developed muscle system around the head. Ants are an important food of the green woodpecker, and anthills are commonly broken open by birds searching for ant grubs and workers. During the winter of 1947 many of these lovely birds died from starvation when the ground and anthills were frozen.

The nestholes made by woodpeckers are often taken over by other birds in subsequent years. They provide an important source of sites for those species which cannot or do not make their own nests. Starlings, tits and nuthatches are common inhabitants of such tree holes, but as the hole enlarges with age and decay, stock doves and small owls may use them. The lesser spotted woodpecker excavates feeding and nesting holes in decaying wood, but the other woodpeckers often bore into solid wood, even telegraph poles and farm timbers, to make their nestholes.

Two other birds commonly feed on insects under bark, the treecreeper *Certhia familiaris* and the wryneck *Jynx torquilla*, which is a member of the woodpecker family. The latter is now a summer resident in parts of southeast England but has recently been found nesting in the Highlands of Scotland; during the last century it was common over all Britain but since then its European range has been steadily contracting. The treecreeper, with its slender, down-curved bill, is often seen running up trees and probing under the bark. When it reaches the upper branches it descends and starts at the base of another tree. Neither of these birds drill nestholes. The wryneck uses old treeholes, and the treecreeper makes its tiny nest behind a piece of loose bark or in a crevice. Since the introduction of Californian redwoods to Britain, the treecreeper often shapes a cranny in the soft pliable bark of the redwood to roost in during winter, well camouflaged against predators.

The woodpeckers, Picidae, (*top*) are well adapted to an arboreal way of life, and the roller *Coracias garrulus* (*bottom right*) is an annual vagrant, usually seen on passage in eastern England. The kingfisher *Alcedo atthis* (*bottom left*) is a resident of streams and rivers, feeding especially on minnows and other small fish.

Pl. 2

Wryneck. Green Woodpecker.

esser Spotted Woodpecker ♂ & ♀. Great Spotted Woodpecker (adult ♂ & young).

Long-tailed Titmouse.
Marsh-Titmouse.
Great Titmouse
Bearded Titmouse.
♂ & ♀
Crested Titmouse
Blue Titmouse

Tits

To alleviate competition for nest sites and food, each species of bird has its own habitat which may be separated in time or space from those of other species. In the woodlands the closely related tits compete for a limited number of nest sites, but differences in feeding habits and habitat preferences reduce interspecific competition. Only the long-tailed tit *Aegithalus caudatus* does not nest in holes or crevices. This tit makes a complex domed nest covered with cobwebs, hair and lichens in trees and bushes. The willow tit *Parus montanus* and crested tit *P. cristatus* both excavate holes in rotting trees and stumps for nests, the former in broadleaved and the latter in coniferous woodlands. The blue tit *P. caeruleus*, great tit *P. major*, marsh tit *P. palustris* and coal tit *P. ater*, along with other woodlands birds, compete for natural tree holes and crevices as nesting sites. Such concealed nests provide protection against predators and bad weather, and thus increase the chances of chick survival. Larger broods are raised and the growth rate of the chicks need not be as fast as it must be with open-nesting species.

Competition for food is reduced between tit species by their feeding at different strata within the woodland vegetation. During the summer months, when their insect food is usually abundant, competition is minimal and the stratification in feeding is less marked. At other times this stratification becomes more noticeable. The heavier, stouter-billed great tit predominantly searches the ground and low shrubs for insects and berries, while the small, agile blue tits and coal tits may be seen in the upper canopy and swaying branches. Marsh tits tend to feed in the lower shrub layers, the long-tailed tit in the higher layers, the woodland edge and the nearby hedgerows.

Blue tits are more a broadleaved woodland species, found especially among oaks. The smallest British tit, the coal tit, prefers narrow-leaved trees, the spruces, pines and larches. The British crested tit breeds solely in the coniferous woodlands of north-east Scotland, varying its diet of insects with pine and juniper seeds in the autumn and winter months.

All the tits are highly territorial during the breeding season, when each pair aggressively defends its territory against other birds. Family groups persist for some time after the fledglings leave the nest, until they are completely independent. These groups break up at night as individual birds roost in the canopy and upper branches, but reform at dawn. Eventually the young disperse to different areas and form flocks with other juveniles. In winter tits group into flocks during the daytime, often with other species of tits, treecreepers, goldcrests and other small songbirds. These move around local areas searching the ground, trees and shrubs for overwintering invertebrates, seeds and berries. It is thought that members of these flocks have greater success in finding food than those searching separately, an important factor for survival during hard winters.

Opposite These illustrations of the titmice, Paridae, show each bird among the vegetation where it is typically found. The crested and bearded tits are uncommon and restricted in distribution.

Right A study of a blue tit *Parus caeruleus* clinging to a bough.

Pl. 6.

Subalpine Warbler.
Dartford Warbler.
Wood-wren
Willow-Wren
Yellow-browed Warbler
Pallas's Willow-Warbler
Greenish Willow-Warbler
Chiffchaff

Warblers

The warblers found in woodlands are mainly shrub- and tree-feeding birds, but owing to their shy habits and small size, they are rarely noticed. All the British warblers are insectivorous, and all except four are summer visitors. The Dartford warbler *Sylvia undata* and Cetti's warbler *Cettia cetti* are both residents but found only in the south of England. Some chiffchaffs *Phylloscopus collybita* winter in the southwest and blackcaps *Sylvia atricapilla* are now also reported in winter. The rest winter south of the Sahara in the savannahs of central Africa. These birds arrive in Britain during April and May, the males coming first to take up territories. These are usually a few hundred square metres in size – quite small compared with the territories of other songbirds. The females arrive later and pair up with males as they enter their territories.

In this warbler plate Thorburn illustrates four species which are rare vagrants to Britain. The sub-alpine warbler *Sylvia cantillans* has sometimes been observed, mainly during the spring migration period. Pallas's willow warbler *Phylloscopus proregulus*, the greenish willow warbler *P. trochiloides* and the yellow-browed warbler *P. inornatus* are sometimes seen on the east and south coasts during the autumn migration.

The two most common warblers, the willow warbler or willow wren *P. trochilus* and the chiffchaff *P. collybita*, are both found on the edges of broadleaved woodlands, but have colonized with equal success commons and gardens where there are mature trees and well-developed bushes and ground vegetation. These and the wood warbler or wood wren *P. sibilatrix* all make enclosed domed nests, a characteristic of this genus of warblers. Chiffchaffs' nests are built above ground in dense vegetation; willow warblers and wood warblers build their nests on or near the ground in dense and sparse herbage respectively. The birds feed on insects in the shrubs and trees, taking caterpillars, flies, beetles and aphids from the leaves and twigs. Sometimes two broods of chicks are raised, each taking about a month from laying to fledging.

The warblers of the genus *Sylvia* differ in one main respect from the *Phylloscopus* warblers: their nests are shaped like an open cup, built in dense shrubs on or near the ground. All show strong territorial behaviour and resemble the other warblers in feeding habits.

Opposite Although similar in size, the warblers show great variation in colouration and song. The Dartford warbler *Sylvia undata* (*middle left*) has declined continually over the last 100 years through habitat destruction, bird collectors and severe winters. There are only a handful of breeding pairs left in southern England.

Above A sketch of a wren *Troglodytes troglodytes* singing. This tiny bird is extremely active, and can often be taken for a mouse as it forages in litter on the ground. It also catches insects among vegetation like a warbler. Its song, which is a prolonged, breathless jingle of trills, can be heard all year.

Ground-feeding birds

Of the ground-feeding birds, blackbirds *Turdus merula* and songthrushes *T. philomelos* are the most common, seen in gardens and woodlands. Blackbirds feed chiefly on earthworms and slugs, but take insects and insect larvae, berries, fruits and seeds; unlike songthrushes, blackbirds can not smash snails. These ground-feeding birds nest in shrubs, in contrast to the willow and wood warblers, which nest on the ground and feed in the shrub layer.

The spread of the blackbird from woodlands to towns started in the last century in Britain, and by 1920 this bird had become a common inhabitant of gardens and parks. The trend has since been repeated in Europe, gradually spreading eastwards to reach Czechoslovakia and Hungary at the present time. In Britain today the blackbird and chaffinch rank equally as the second most common resident birds; the wren tops this list.

The wagtails represent another group of ground-living birds often seen in the lowlands. The pied wagtail *Motacilla alba*, the grey wagtail *M. cinerea* and the yellow wagtail *M. flava* are all closely associated with water. The pied wagtail is, like the songbirds, a daytime feeder, continually searching for both flying and ground-dwelling insects in grassland and by the edges of streams and ponds. It is more associated with man than the other two wagtails, and is nowadays most commonly seen around gardens and parks. At night time it sometimes forms communal roosts, like starlings, in trees and on buildings. The increase in urban wastelands over the last 50 years has provided yet another habitat for these ground-feeding birds.

The ring ouzel *Turdus torquatus* (*left*) and blackbird *T. merula* (*right*). The ring ouzel is a summer-breeding resident widespread throughout Scotland especially on moors and heathlands. It is absent from southeast and eastern England.

These urban wastelands are providing a new sort of habitat for many bird species. Defunct coal and railway depots, gas-works and rubbish tips mean undisturbed areas where weeds and seed-bearing plants thrive and insects abound. Wintering flocks of meadow pipits, sparrows, skylarks and finches are frequent visitors to these new feeding sites. Occasionally a stonechat or great grey shrike may appear, and a few redpolls may also be seen, if seeds are available.

Above The wagtails, Motacillidae.
Below right The pied wagtail *Motacilla alba* is often seen on pasture and meadows, and near buildings in the breeding season.
Below left The mistle thrush *Turdus viscivorus*. This bird is also known as the storm-cock from its custom of singing wildly during early spring gales.

Owls

The owls contrast markedly with the fast-flying raptors, the hawks and falcons, for they have a loose, soft plumage that allows them to make a quiet and slow approach to their prey. Their characteristic form is easily recognizable and is adapted to nocturnal hunting. The large forward-facing eyes are well suited to night vision, and especially sharp at detecting movement. Although they have little sense of smell, the owl's hearing is extraordinarily acute. A barn owl can detect and catch mice in total darkness. The ear tufts on the short-eared owl *Asio flammeus* and the long-eared owl *A. otus* are just feather tufts, and have nothing to do with hearing.

In England and Wales, the tawny owl *Strix aluco* is the only common breeding owl in the broadleaved woodlands. It is generally found in mature woodlands, and more recently in wooded parks and gardens. No nest is built, and the eggs are layed on debris, in an old tree hole or even a burrow in the ground. Where there is a thick cover of vegetation bank voles are heavily preyed on by tawny owls, while small birds are only a minor food source. The opposite is true in towns, where the sparrow makes up half the owls' diet, and small mammals are relatively unimportant.

The two eared owls feed mainly on small mammals, the short-eared specializing in field voles. The barn owl *Tyto alba* shows a surprising penchant for shrews, which are disliked by most predators. Breeding success and the number of chicks reared are closely linked with the abundance of prey. The numbers of the short-eared owl fluctuate with the three to four year cycle of vole abundance. During the vole plagues of 1890 to 1892, the short-eared owl rapidly increased in numbers, even raising two broods per pair each year, instead of one. When the vole numbers 'crashed', most of these owls died of starvation. A breeding pair of barn owls requires about 3000 small mammals per year for food, and half of these are usually field voles. But the owl's diet often contains other prey. By analysing the owl's disgorged pellets of fur, bone and feather, one can find remains of small birds and of large insects such as moths and cockchafers. The small vagrant scops owl *Otus scops* feeds almost entirely on insects, while half the diet of the little owl *Athene noctua*, an introduced species, is composed of insects.

The eared owls breed mainly in the north of Britain and may disperse south in winter. The short-eared owl both nests and feeds on open moor and heathlands. This owl's main prey, the field vole, has increased dramatically in the thick undergrowth of young conifer plantations, spreading from there to surrounding grasslands and thus boosting the short-eared owls' food supply. The long-eared owl, though it may nest occasionally on marshes and dunes, is more a resident of coniferous woods. Occasionally nests are made on the ground or in a burrow, but more often the abandoned nest of a crow or magpie is used. The afforestation of large areas has therefore helped both species of eared owls, through increasing the abundance of prey and, with the long-eared owl, providing more suitable breeding areas.

The wanton slaughter of little owls earlier this century was based on the myth that these owls took gamebirds. It has now been shown that the little owl is an important predator of mice, voles and young rats, rarely taking gamebirds or poultry. Legal protection from persecution has helped the little owl, but the disappearance of suitable nesting sites is now as great a threat to this species as pesticide poisoning was twenty years ago.

The long-eared owl *Asio otus* (*top left*), tawny owl *Strix aluco* (*top right*), short-eared owl *A. flammeus* (*bottom right*) and barn owl *Tyto alba* (*bottom left*). The owls contrast markedly with the hawks. Their soft, loose plumage allows them to make a quiet and slow approach to their prey in twilight and at night.

Long-eared Owl.   Tawny Owl.
Barn-Owl   Short-eared Owl.

Sparrow-Hawk. (♂ & ♀)

Goshawk (adult & young)

Short-winged Hawks

Once the hawk of princes, the goshawk *Accipiter gentilis* is now the species most commonly used in falconry in Britain, being more effective against larger game and birds than the peregrine. This short-winged hawk was once a regular inhabitant of Britain, but like the osprey was persecuted to extinction by the beginning of this century. Each breeding pair requires 5000 hectares, of which a third must be mature woodland. Only 16 per cent of the British land area was wooded in 1700, and this was further reduced to five per cent by the early 1800s. Fragmentation of these woodlands destroyed the goshawks' breeding haunts, whereas the smaller sparrowhawk *A. nisus* survived.

The goshawk population is increasing slowly in Britain, probably from adults lost or released by falconers. Although the plantations established by the forestry commission over the last few decades have now reached maturity, this bird has not increased as other birds of prey have done.

Both the sparrowhawk and goshawk rely upon an element of surprise in catching their prey. Sight, speed and skill in flying are all well developed and, like the other raptors, the sense of smell is poor or absent. The long legs and long needle-like talons enable the prey to be taken in woodland and thick vegetation as well as in the open. The male sparrowhawk is only half the weight of the female, and takes small birds with ease. In woodland the goshawk will prey upon woodpigeons and rooks, while in open countryside pheasants, rabbits and even hares are taken.

Unlike the falcons, sparrowhawks build their own nests. These are made of sticks and twigs in trees, usually in dense coniferous or broadleaved woodland. The male bird brings prey to the nest for the female and young. During one year, a breeding pair will need to kill about 70 kilograms of prey, the equivalent of 2,000 small birds.

The most common of the day-hunting raptors, the sparrowhawk, sometimes reaches two breeding pairs per square kilometre, but the restricted number of nest sites tends to limit breeding densities. The numbers of these birds have now recovered from the adverse effects of organochlorine pesticides such as Aldrin and Dieldrin, which were widely used in the 1950s and 60s and which are particularly harmful because their residues persist in the soil. In farming areas, the average number of young reared each year was four per pair before 1951, but thereafter this decreased to less than two per pair. There was no corresponding decrease in non-farming areas. It is now believed that the sparrowhawks are not important predators of gamebirds and their persecution by farmers and gamekeepers is diminishing.

Opposite Sparrowhawk *Accipiter nisus* (*top*) and goshawk *A. gentilis* (*below*). The sparrowhawk is distinguished from other small birds of prey by its short rounded wings and long tail. The goshawk has broad-based wings which often look pointed except when it is soaring.
Right A goshawk on a bow-perch.

Wetland Wildlife

The British wetlands provide a wide range of habitats, from the deep lochs and small tarns of the Highlands to the lush rivers and ponds of southern England. A varied array of resident and migrant birds are to be found in these throughout the year. The importance of Britain as an over-wintering area for many of the north European and arctic wildfowl is now recognized. Various sites are preserved and protected by local and national ornithological organizations. The destruction of marshes and fens by man has, to some extent, been compensated by the creation of lakes, canals, reservoirs and gravel pits. These new habitats have been and are being colonized by many wildfowl and grebes.

The three indigenous freshwater mammals – otters, water shrews and water voles – have been joined by escapees from fur-farms: coypu, mink and, for a while, musk rat.

Divers

Divers and grebes are the only two groups of freshwater diving birds. Although unrelated, they bear many superficial resemblances, due to convergent evolution, in aquatic adaptations and courtship displays. Both groups winter on inshore estuaries and coastal areas when they are coloured drab browns and greys like the juveniles. The colourful breeding plumages are seen in summer when these birds are on upland lochs and tarns, or in lowland lakes and ponds.

All the divers have arctic or sub-arctic distributions and usually migrate in winter, from the freshwater breeding grounds, southwards to the inshore coastal areas and estuaries of central and southern Europe.

There are two resident divers in Britain: the red-throated diver *Gavia stellata* and the black-throated diver *G. arctica*. Although one or two pairs of red-throated divers breed in Ireland, both species are mainly restricted to the freshwater lochs and tarns in northwest Scotland during the breeding season. The red-throated diver alone breeds in the Shetland and Orkney Isles. Disturbance by man in the nineteenth century caused a decrease in population of both species, but since 1951 their numbers have increased again, with some colonization of southwest Scotland by the black-throated diver.

The black-throated diver breeds on deep-water lochs and selects a nesting site such as an islet or peninsula within one metre of the water's edge and inaccessible to predators. The absence of emergent vegetation is a critical factor for habitat selection; the opposite is true for the grebes. The red-throated diver requires smaller and shallower pools for breeding, but also nests on shore close to water. It may have to fly to nearby deeper lakes or coastal areas to feed as the breeding pools do not always support the fish and invertebrates it requires.

Divers eat fish, crustaceans and molluscs which are caught during fast underwater dives. The black-throated diver has been recorded diving for up to five minutes at a depth of 100 metres; on average, though, most dives last a minute. The webbed feet are set well back and so provide propulsion; the wings are used for navigation.

The great northern diver *G. immer* from Greenland and Iceland is seen around Britain's coasts both in winter and summer, notably in northwest Scotland where it is commonly mistaken for the slightly smaller black-throated diver. The white-billed diver *G. adamsii* is slightly larger than the great northern and is a rare winter vagrant.

The great northern diver *Gavia immer* (*top*), the red-throated diver *G. stellata* (*middle left*), the white-billed diver *G. adamsii* (*middle right*) and the black-throated diver *G. artica* (*bottom*). The winter plumage of all divers is duller than when they come inland in the spring to breed on freshwater lochs.

Great Northern Diver (summer & winter).

ed-throated Diver. (summer & winter).

White-billed Northern Diver.

Pl.

Black-necked or Eared Grebe.
Red-necked Grebe. Great Crested Grebe.

Grebes

Man has changed the face of East Anglia over the last thousand years. 350 years of peat cutting which began in the tenth century produced the Broads as we know them today. Their formation involved the removal of 25 million cubic metres of peat. Vast drainage and land reclamation schemes had devastated most of the reed and rush fens by the mid-eighteenth century. The black tern and Savi's warbler consequently disappeared. The population of great crested grebe *Podiceps cristatus* was also affected by these changes though it suffered other pressures. The Victorian millinery trade with an eye for fashion used its silky breast plumage, and, helped by egg collectors and specimen hunters, the grebe population was reduced to 42 pairs by 1860. The sight of its fantastic courtship displays belonged to an earlier generation. Legal protection instigated in 1869 arrested its decline and that of many other birds which have since gradually increased in distribution and numbers. The development of gravel pits and reservoirs has provided new breeding grounds for many of our wetland birds in the last 40 years. In 1965 the great crested grebe numbered over 2000 breeding pairs in Britain – double the number in 1931. The grebes have generally a more southerly distribution than the divers and nest in the thick vegetation around the margins of still and slow-moving waters.

The grebes are a cosmopolitan bird family which have increased markedly in number and range over the last century. The Slavonian grebe *P. auritus* and black-necked grebe *P. nigricollis* were winter residents and passage migrants last century. Both have subsequently bred and maintained colonies throughout the summer in Scotland, though the breeding areas have changed. The black-necked grebe colonized parts of Britain and Wales for a number of years, and Ireland from 1915 to 1957. Only the little grebe or dabchick *Tachybaptus ruficollis* remains essentially a freshwater bird in winter. The others usually move to sheltered inshore coastal waters and estuaries as the lakes and ponds freeze, and join other grebes migrating to the shores of Britain from northwest Europe. Moulting takes place in the autumn, when the summer plumage that Thorburn illustrates gives way to the brown, grey and white feathers of the winter birds.

Like the divers, the grebes are well adapted to underwater swimming, but the wings are held tightly against the body and the partially webbed feet are used for navigation. When disturbed, like the divers they sink under the surface or perform a small forward jump upon diving. The great crested grebe may dive to a depth of 30 metres during winter, though a dive of two to four metres lasting 30 seconds is average. This grebe is predominantly a fish eater all year round, but will take insects, molluscs and larvae. Small food is eaten underwater, while larger fish are dealt with on the surface, the head being eaten first. The little grebe feeds on insects, larvae, molluscs, crustaceans and small fish when available.

The black-necked grebe *Podiceps nigricollis* (*top*), the red-necked grebe *P. griseigena* (*middle left*), the great crested grebe *P. cristatus* (*middle right*), the Slavonian grebe *P. auritus* (*bottom left*) and the little grebe or dabchick *Tachybaptus ruficollis* (*bottom right*). The grebes are increasing markedly in range and number.

Pl

Harriers

The harriers' polygamous nature is a unique feature which distinguishes them from other birds of prey. Male hen harriers *Circus cyaneus* may have up to seven female mates and keep them and their young supplied with prey till the offspring are partly grown. Montagu's harrier *C. pygargus* is the smallest and least polygamous species, there being usually one female, or at the most two, associated with each male.

The drainage of the East Anglian fens from the seventh century onwards led to widespread destruction of the dense reedbeds – the breeding, living and roosting habitat of both the marsh harrier *C. aeruginosus* and often Montagu's harrier. Further reduced through persecution by gamekeepers, they became rare birds and, as such, received the attention of egg and skin collectors last century. Both species were extinct in England by the turn of the century.

Immigrant marsh harriers bred occasionally over the following 50 years and had become regular breeders in Dorset by 1951 and at Minsmere in Suffolk by 1955. A peak of 18 breeding pairs was reached by 1958 in East Anglia, but declined to between three and six in the early 1970s. High levels of organochlorine pesticides were found in dead birds in the early 1960s, and this has been named as a major cause of decline in the harriers and many other birds of prey. Adult breeding birds of the marsh harrier reside in Britain. The young are migratory for the first two years of their life, moving to Africa for the winter. Like the other harriers, there is a high mortality rate because many are shot during their passage through southern Europe and Spain, and it is this which now mainly reduces the European populations.

Montagu's harrier is wholly migratory and is even more susceptible than the marsh harrier to this shooting. In Norfolk there are no regular breeding birds left on the marshes, and only one or two pairs now breed on West Country moors.

The hen harrier has spread across Scotland during this century despite continued illegal persecution by gamekeepers. They were formerly abundant on the northern moors of Britain, until gamebird preservation became important last century and pole-trapping started to catch large numbers. Afforestation greatly helped the hen harriers by the provision of protected areas and thick undergrowth for nest sites. This coupled with its polygamous habits enabled the harrier to increase continually both in numbers and distribution. The hen harrier was the only British bird of prey to increase its population and distribution during the 1960s when all the others were severely affected by high pesticide residues.

Opposite Montagu's harrier *Circus pygargus* (*top left*), the hen harrier *C. cyaneus* (*top right*) and the marsh harrier *C. aeruginosus* (*bottom*). The harriers are the only polygamous birds of prey.
Right A sketch taken from life of a male hen harrier in immature plumage.

The glossy ibis *Plegadis falcinellus* (*top left*), the night heron *Nycticorax nycticorax* (*top right*), the squacco heron *Ardeola ralloides* (*middle right*), the little bittern *Ixobrychus minutus* (*middle left*), the American bittern *Botaurus lentiginosus* (*bottom right*) and the bittern *B. stellaris* (*bottom left*).

Herons

The long-legged, freshwater, wading birds are a feature of Thorburn's bird paintings, although only the grey heron *Ardea cinerea* was a British resident at that time. This bird, with a wingspan of up to two metres, only weighs one to two kilogrammes. This represents an adaptation to soaring, wide dispersal and escape from predators. Unlike the continental herons, the British ones do not migrate each year; instead, they disperse locally away from their communal nesting grounds or 'heronries'.

In winter the British population is strengthened by Scandinavian passage visitors. It is at this time of year that fish constitute the main source

The cattle egret *Bubulcus ibis* (*top left*), the purple heron *Ardea purpurea* (*top right*), the great egret *Egretta alba* (*bottom right*), the heron *Ardea cinerea* (*bottom left*) and the little egret *Egretta garzetta* (*middle left*). All have long, probing bills, ideal for catching fish.

of food, and occasionally herons frequent protected fishing waters – much to the objection of anglers. Some persecution of these birds occurs in parts of Europe, although there is now widespread legal protection for the species. During the summer, frogs, snakes, small rodents, birds, insects and shrimps are eaten when available. The main factor in controlling the British populations is the occasional severe winter: that of 1962 to 1963 is an example, when the population dwindled to 2250 pairs by the following spring. Generally the population averages around 4000 nests.

The night heron *Nycticorax nycticorax*, purple heron *A. purpurea* and little egret *Egretta garzetta* are all annual vagrants to our southern and

Pl. 4

Bewick's Swan.   Whooper Swan.

Mute Swan (adult & young)

southeastern shores, possibly as a result of their over-shooting their normal breeding grounds during migration. The Squacco heron *Ardeola ralloides*, cattle egret *Bubulcus ibis* and great white egret *Egretta alba* are rare vagrants, though some have been imported to commercial wildlife parks. Flamingos *Phoenicopterus ruber* have occasionally escaped such parks and have taken to living on the muddy shores of the eastern coast of Britain.

The bittern *Botaurus stellaris* is closely related to the herons, but is distinguished by the cryptic plumage and characteristic 'bittern-stance' posture when alarmed. These secretive creatures are most often espied in thick reed beds or vegetation around water, especially in the protected marshes of the Fens and the northwest of England. Like herons, the bittern's diet is predominantly animal food, including frogs, birds, voles and fish. From late winter to midsummer male bitterns may be heard booming warnings to other males to leave their females alone. The male takes no part in incubating or rearing and he may have up to five females in his territory. Although extinct in 1866 due to wetland drainage and persecution immigrant bitterns have bred in Norfolk since 1911 and spread from there to other areas.

The American bittern is a rare vagrant from the Americas, unlike the little bittern *Ixobrychus minutus* which may in the future colonize our east coast wetlands, where it is an annual passage migrant from the expanding Dutch and Rhine delta colonies.

Wildfowl

The now famous Bewick's swan *Cygnus columbianus* was named after the famous eighteenth century illustrator, Thomas Bewick. Like the whooper swan *C. cygnus*, it migrates from northern breeding grounds to Britain in the autumn and overwinters on the wet marshlands.

Bewick's swans *Cygnus columbianus* (*top left*) and whooper swans *C. cygnus* (*top right and flock behind*) are both winter visitors to England from their breeding grounds in the arctic and boreal forests of northern Asia. The mute swan *C. olor* (*below*) is a natural British resident and not a feral introduction as previously supposed.

The bills are strong and adapted for grazing both aquatic and terrestrial plants. Fast flowing deep waters are avoided.

The Bewick's swan's wintering ranges changed earlier this century. Scotland was the main wintering ground until the 1930s when it gradually gave way to selected English sites. One of these sites was at the Slimbridge Wildfowl Trust reserve. Now 1500 Bewick's winter in England – a quarter of the European population. By mid-March most have left to return via the Baltic to the tundra breeding grounds in the Asian arctic. The whooper breeds further south in the boreal forest zones of north Asia. The British winter visitors come from the Icelandic breeding grounds; around 2500 disperse to the Wash and north Britain, and about 2000 fly to Ireland. They were traditionally hunted by the Icelanders for their down.

Since the Middle Ages, the mute swan *C. olor* has been semi-domesticated in many of Britain's waterways. Swans enjoyed protection from royalty for whom they were decorative and provided meat. This century has seen a massive spread of these beautiful, large; white birds throughout Europe, especially due to the release of many semi-domesticated birds since the last war. Fossil evidence shows that the mute swan is a natural British resident. Unlike the whooper and smaller Bewick's swans, the mute seldom migrates in western Europe. Local movements are usually less than 50 kilometres and stay within the same river system. The characteristic knob on the bill enlarges in the male during the breeding season, when he will aggressively defend the brood from predators.

All swans and geese have a well-developed social grouping; the young remain with the parents over the first winter and spring and may unite in subsequent breeding seasons and migrations. Pair bonding is strong and non-seasonal, often lasting all through the breeding life. Gregarious behaviour is common outside the breeding season the mute swan being a possible exception: in this species the breeding pairs remain separate, but there are non-breeding herds throughout the year. Large aggregations of geese

The brent goose *Branta bernicla* (*top left*), the barnacle goose *B. leucopsis* (*top right*), the snow goose *Anser caerulescens* (*bottom right*) and the red-breasted goose *B. ruficollis* (*bottom left*). Although the snow goose is a rare vagrant to the British Isles, it is not as rare as the red-breasted goose seen only 24 times since 1776.

occur around Britain during their winter stay, sometimes numbering several thousands. At times they feed on crops, doing considerable damage.

The greylag goose *Anser anser* is the only native breeding goose in Britain, but breeding greylags became extinct in the English fens early last century, and in Ireland in the 1700s. Twenty-five years ago the species was restricted to the Outer Hebrides, but with man's help this ancestor

The white-fronted goose *Anser albifrons* (*top left*), the grey lag goose *A. anser* (*top right*), the bean goose *A. fabalis* (*bottom right*) and the pink-footed goose *A. brachrhynchus* (*bottom left*). In the background is a gaggle of greylags and the familiar 'V' flight formation.

of the domesticated goose has colonized parts of Scotland, and some localities in England. Feral birds continue to extend this range southwards.

Of the grey geese, the white-fronted goose *A. albifrons* is the commonest winter resident. Flying by day and night with regular stopovers at traditional nesting sites, they arrive at the British estuaries and saltmarshes in October along with the pink-footed geese *A. brachyrhynchus* and declining numbers of bean geese *A. fabalis*. At high tide, the geese move to the marshes and fields to feed, while at low tide they are often seen grazing on estuarine grasses and roots. Later in the winter, cultivated fields are more frequently visited, both to graze grass and to take grain, green vegetables and root crops.

The snow goose *A. caerulescens* and the red-breasted goose *Branta ruficollis* are both rare winter vagrants to Britain.

The only sea goose that frequents Britain is the Brent goose *B. bernicla*, large flocks of which fill the eastern coastal skies in long lines in autumn. Up to 20,000 Russian birds now winter on the English east and south coasts and roost on the sea. About the same number of birds winter in Ireland but these come from Greenland and Canada. During the 1930s their main food, eelgrass, was seriously depleted through disease on the North Sea shores, causing a considerable decrease in the number of birds coming to these areas each winter. The numbers have since increased to reach over 80,000 at the present.

The Canada goose *B. canadensis* is related to the smaller and migratory Brent and barnacle geese *B. leucopsis*, but was introduced to Britain only 300 years ago. Britain is its main European stronghold with now over 20,000 birds. Expansion and introduction of this easily tamed goose has led to colonies forming in Scandinavia. Here the geese are migratory unlike the British population which is resident. Like the *Anser* geese, it feeds on plant food, especially grass roots and seeds.

Unlike swans and geese, ducks show a marked sexual dimorphism in plumage. The bright breeding plumage of the male is especially well developed in the temperate regions, and contrasts markedly with the dull camouflaging colours of the female. Iridescent, metallic colours are common on the wing, and are present all year. Outside the breeding and courting seasons, the male usually moults to the sombre colours of the female.

Of the shelduck group, only the common shelduck *Tadorna tadorna* breeds around Britain's coasts. The sand and mudflats provide rich feeding grounds for these wading ducks. Small shellfish constitute a major part of the food, especially *Hydrobia ulvae*, but other snails and some green seaweeds are also eaten. In summer the breeding ducks leave their grounds throughout northern Europe and congregate for their annual moult in the Wadensee area in Germany. As many as 100,000 gather there, leaving the juveniles at the breeding grounds. The Irish shelducks which number a few thousand congregate in Bridgwater Bay in Somerset.

Only one perching duck, the mandarin *Aix galericulata*, is found in Britain. It was introduced from the East early this century. Like many ducks, it successfully lives in ornamental lakes and ponds, and occasionally escapes to set up new colonies.

Of the dabbling ducks, the most widespread is the mallard *Anas platyrhynchos*. Altogether there are probably over one and a half millions in western Europe. The British population of 150,000 pairs is swelled in winter by large numbers of immigrants from north and east Europe. The most omnivorous and opportunistic of all ducks, the mallard, breeds and lives in small ponds, inshore coastal areas, man-made lakes and highland tarns.

The gadwall *Anas strepera* is a recent addition to England. First being introduced to Norfolk in 1950, it has spread, through further introductions and escapes, to other counties. But in Scotland and Ireland the small breeding population is believed to be natural. Icelandic pintail ducks migrate to Britain for the winter, while the British birds fly to the western Mediterranean. Russian and Finnish pintails may number over a quarter of a million in the Mediterranean and the Black Sea in winter. The most migratory ducks of all are the garganeys which make the journey from all over western Europe and Russia to their winter grounds south of the Sahara.

A coastal scene with mallards *Anas platyrhynchos* (*top left*), gadwalls *A. strepera* (*top right*), a shelduck *Tadorna tadorna* (*bottom right*) and a ruddy shelduck (*bottom left*). The sands and mudflats provide rich feeding grounds for these wading ducks.

Mallard (♂&♀) Gadwall. (♂&♀)

Ruddy Sheld-Duck. Common Sheld-Duck.

A. Thorburn
1918

Otter

Hunting for pleasure or gain has been a characteristic of western society from prehistoric times to the present. One of the earliest evidences of otter hunting is an otter skin chair from a Bronze Age royal grave in Denmark. Over the last 1000 years in Britain only one freshwater mammal, the beaver *Castor fiber*, has been lost through over-hunting. The beaver has survived in parts of Europe, Asia and America, but hunting for its valuable fur was the major cause of its near-extinction in the Americas. Control of beaver hunting was introduced in this century, and it now inhabits many of its former haunts. In Britain it survived into the twelfth century in Wales, when Giraldus records this giant rodent dam-building on only one river in the country.

The otter *Lutra lutra* has been heavily blamed for destroying fish stocks and nets and has suffered persecution by gamekeepers. The growth of otter hunts last century took their toll on this sleek water mammal. Despite this, otter numbers are believed to have remained stable for 150 years and have only declined severely since the 1950s. Then the most drastic reductions were in the Midlands and the Scottish lowlands where man's influence on the environment had a greater impact on wildlife than his predation on animals directly. Agricultural and industrial pollution was rife and encroachment on the waterways by water authorities, fishermen and sports was on the increase. In recent years, action of water-controlling bodies has led to marked reductions in waterway disturbance and pollution, but there is as yet no evidence that the otter is increasing to its former levels. Its long-term survival could be ensured by setting up otter havens.

Although primarily inhabitants of freshwater, some otters live permanently on coasts, where

The long, flattened body, tapering tail, short legs and broad, webbed feet of the otter *Lutra lutra* are well adapted to an aquatic environment. A full-grown male will measure 105–120 cm from nose to tail-tip. Otters retreat into their holts by day, and emerge at dusk to prey on frogs and fishes.

they feed on fish and crabs. It has emerged that the otter, like many of the British carnivores, is an opportunist, catching the most easily available food. Weak and slow fish are removed from commercial trout and salmon streams, thereby enhancing the stock for sport. It also takes crayfish, but is renowned for indiscriminate killing, in slow water and lakes, well in excess of its normal food requirements. This is a trait exhibited by other members of the weasel group on land.

Water vole

It is curious that Thorburn illustrated the black variety of the water vole *Arvicola terrestris*. This variety is restricted to parts of East Anglia and northwest Scotland while the commoner brown variety ranges across Britain, Europe and Asia as far as Lake Baikal. Despite the Latin description 'terrestris', this rodent is an inhabitant of the edges of rivers, canals and ponds where it feeds and breeds among the rushes and reeds. It is easily distinguished from the other voles by its large size and aquatic habits, and is an expert swimmer, diving to the security of an underwater burrow entrance at the slightest sign of danger. This behaviour and the presence of its burrow entrances above water-level are the main indications that it is present, and a closer inspection of the reedbeds will reveal its feeding areas and latrines. The water vole has a curious way of feeding. First it will cut lengths of large round reeds and bring them to its feeding platform, cut in the middle of a reedbed. Then, in the manner of the beaver, it selects the thinner end in its forepaws and peels the reed from end to end. Only when the inner pith is totally exposed will it consume its fare. Like many other rodents it is an ubiquitous feeder taking a wide range of plants, bark, rhizomes and sometimes dead fish. The early Victorians blamed it for attacking fish stocks but this has never been substantiated, though at times it was a pest of the wetland osier beds, feeding on the bark, buds and shoots of the trees during periods of bad weather.

The water vole is now fairly common in the lowlands of Britain but, with the influence of the rapacious mink and stoat, its numbers never seem to reach epidemic proportions. Even pike have been known to take this vole. But its highest mortality occurs in the nest when often only one or two young survive from a litter of five. After leaving the nest at 14 days old, the life expectancy is only about six months. In common with other voles, the water vole will give birth to a number of litters between spring and autumn and can successfully mate directly after the birth of a litter, thus producing the next 20 to 22 days later. But the limits of population size appear to be determined by winter food supplies.

It is absent from Ireland, as is the field vole *Microtus agrestis*. Occasionally the water vole is mistaken for the brown rat which also swims in waterways. It is easily distinguished from the rat which has a longer snout and a long, hairless tail. Furthermore, voles rarely frequent areas where rats are present.

Escapes from fur-farms

Fur-farming was a lucrative trade earlier this century and escapes of these mammals sometimes resulted in successful colonizations in Britain. Nearly all these mammals are associated with water. Their pelt is densely packed, water-repellent and soft, equally fine attributes for an aquatic existence or a fur coat. The musk rat *Ondatra zibethicus* is a large American relative of the water vole and became a temporary member of the British fauna in the 1930s following its escape from fur-farms. It caused serious concern because of its damage to river banks, and the dams it built, and was successfully exterminated in 1937. Only two introductions now cause any trouble. These are the American mink and the coypu.

The coypu *Myocaster coypus* is a large water-dwelling rodent and resembles a cross between a rat and a guinea pig to which it is related. Conspicuous for its webbed hindfeet and size – up to 65 centimetres long and weighing seven kilograms in an adult male – it is now confined to

the marshlands and reedbeds of east Norfolk and Suffolk. About 50 years ago it escaped and spread rapidly to many areas of southern and eastern England causing damage to dykes, river-banks and farmland. Control by trapping and shooting coupled with severe winters led to its extermination in all areas except East Anglia.

Mink are members of the weasel group. It appears that the European mink *Mustela lutreola* never inhabited Britain while its close relative the American mink *M. vison* has bred successfully in many areas of Britain since the first breeding population was recorded in 1956. There appears to be little interaction between the mink and the otter: their habitat and feeding requirements are slightly different although the latter may prey on mink at times. There is also little direct evidence that the mink is damaging the natural wildlife of Britain.

Water voles *Arvicola terrestris* are often confused with the brown rat and wrongly called water rats. The vole's tail is hairier and the snout rounder, and it will swim underwater to burrow in the bank when disturbed. Thorburn depicts the common brown form, and the black found chiefly in northern Scotland and the fens.

Marine Wildlife

The remote and secluded coasts of Britain still remain the major haunt of seabirds in the north-east Atlantic. Millions of birds breed on the rocky cliffs and hills each year, together with seals on the shores of the north and west coasts. Commercial exploitation of seabirds and whales around the coasts has stopped, but changes in population numbers occur from other causes, some known, some unknown. Oil pollution has now become a major problem affecting the animals of the coast, particularly seabirds. Unseen pollution of the sea by persistent chemical wastes is regarded as an even more important problem in some areas. On the other hand, not all seabirds are declining: the expansion of gulls and fulmars this century has been surprising, and is providing scientists and ornithologists with new fields to study.

Whales

Whales are the descendents of land mammals that are thought to have returned to the sea some 70 million years ago. The group includes the largest animal ever recorded: the blue whale or Sibbald's rorqual *Balaenoptera musculus*. The largest recorded blue whale measured 31 metres in length and was taken in Antarctic waters. Despite the size of this creature, it feeds almost exclusively on 'krill'. These are small prawn-like crustacea about five centimetres in length. They are sieved on to the baleen plates when a mouthful of water is forced through these thin, fringed, plates by the tongue. The baleen whales, which include the right whales and rorquals, all utilize this filter-feeding mechanism.

The toothed whales, which include the sperm whale *Physeter catodon* and also the various dolphins and porpoises, feed upon larger animals. The sperm whale is often recovered sporting sucker marks five to six centimetres in diameter

Top Sibbald's rorqual or the blue whale *Balaenoptera musculus* is a baleen whale with throat grooves which hold vast quantities of water for sifting. The flecking is barnacles, which often encrust the creature.
Below The sperm whale *Physeter catodon* is the largest toothed whale, and dives to great depths to catch squid.

Pl

Atlantic Right Whale.

Humpbacked Whale. 1/75

from the giant squid upon which it preys. Examination of the stomach contents of sperm whales has shown that giant squid of up to ten metres long are taken. Toothed whales and baleen whales are not substantially in competition because the two groups thrive on different food sources.

Extreme adaptation of the whales to their aquatic environment is reflected in the hairless smooth skin and streamlined shape. The forelimbs are modified as flippers, while hindlimbs are normally absent. However, one humpback whale *Megaptera novaeangliae* caught off Vancouver Island in 1919 was found to have hindlimbs 1.2 metres in length. The pelvic bones are vestigial, possibly as a streamlining adaptation. The bulk of the propulsive force is exerted by the horizontal tail flukes, moved in a vertical plane. The flippers are used for steering.

These mammals' diving abilities are well known. The sperm whales dive for periods of up to an hour and the body of one of these whales has been found entangled in a submarine cable laid at a depth of 2200 metres. The animals possess various physiological and anatomical adaptations which enable them to dive and acquire a large oxygen debt. This oxygen debt is paid off when the whale surfaces to 'blow' through the blowholes situated on the top of the head. The same adaptations prevent the whale suffering from decompression sickness.

Protection from the cold is afforded by a thick layer of fat held in a network of fibrous tissue beneath the skin. The oil which may be rendered from this blubber has become a major source of profit for whaling companies for several centuries. In the days of the whalebone corset and umbrella, whalebone was also a valuable product, and reached a price of £700 per ton.

Initially man's use of the whale was for the large quantities of meat. Availability was probably the result of accidental strandings. The mass strandings of whales that occasionally take place are still not satisfactorily understood, but are thought to be due to changes in the currents which could alter the distribution of food animals. A high incidence of stranding takes place where whales congregate in coastal waters and causes a significant mortality among some species each year. Stranding is also a seasonal phenomenon in many cases, due to the migration of some species from high latitude feeding grounds in the summer to low latitude areas in the winter, where the water is warmer and where they give birth. The grey whale *Eschrichtius glaucus* congregates in large numbers off the Californian peninsula from January to March spending the summer months in more northerly latitudes.

Where stranding is seasonal and fairly predictable, whales were probably habitually used by man. However, to improve upon the unreliable possibility of a self-beached animal, boats may well have been used to drive animals ashore where they could be readily cut up and utilized. This form of whaling is still practised in the Faroe Islands where the small pilot whale *Globicephala melaena* is taken.

The Basques almost exterminated the black right whale *Eubalena glacialis* off their coasts in medieval times. These slow-moving whales were hunted from small boats using hand-held harpoons. The progressive decline in whale numbers in the Atlantic led eventually to the exploitation of the Greenland right whale *Balaena mysticetus*

Opposite Two baleen whales: the humpbacked *Megaptera novaeangliae* (*bottom*) found throughout the Atlantic and Pacific, and the black right *Eubalaena glacialis*.
Above right The bottlenosed whale *Hyperoodon ampullatus*, found in the North Atlantic as far as the ice margin, has a single pair of teeth, invisible in the living animal.

in more northerly latitudes. This whale became the 'right' whale to catch since it rendered a larger amount of oil than any other. In common with the other right whales and the sperm whale it had the advantage of floating when dead. Furthermore, it was less likely to attack the small boats, which played the animal until it was dead, than was the sperm whale. Many illustrations of encounters with aggressive sperm whales were carved on their extracted teeth, a form of carving known as 'scrimshaw'.

The carcass of a captured whale was taken alongside the mother ship and the blubber removed with long-handled 'flensing' knives. The major part of the carcass was cut adrift and wasted. The blubber was then either rendered into oil in a 'tryworks' on the deck of the vessel or at a shore-based station, as existed at Spitzbergen and Jan Mayen Island. The technique of whaling from a small boat was largely confined to the right and sperm whales. The rorquals were faster swimming and sank when dead, and were thus largely immune from hunters. This lasted until 1860 when Svend Foyn, a Norwegian, perfected the explosive harpoon, fired from a steamer. The steamer could keep pace with the rorquals and also provided a platform from which the dead, hence sinking whale could be hauled to the surface and pumped full of compressed air. The carcass was then towed back to a land slip and rendered into the various products.

Shore-based whaling persisted in Britain until the mid-1920s, but most of the management and skilled labour was carried out by the Norwegians. This was true of the Antarctic region also, where the first whaling station was set up on South Georgia Island in 1904. Since the British Government administered the Falkland Island Dependencies, thanks to Captain Cook claiming them in 1775, it was able to impose regulations upon the industry to prevent over-exploitation of a valuable resource. Licences were required for whaling, and restrictions were imposed upon the number of catcher vessels operating. The levies imposed were used to fund research on whales and by 1935 enough was known to enable the industry to operate on exact knowledge. As a result of this research, licence applications for whaling operations were refused and pelagic whaling using a factory ship was initiated. This allowed the industry to become independent of a shore-based operation.

Each 200,000-ton factory vessel was capable, in conjunction with its satellite fleet of catchers, of completely processing whale carcases at sea. The initial impact of this unrestricted whaling was to produce a glut of oil. The whaling industry was forced to cease fishing for a whole season to allow the market to absorb the surplus.

The lack of restriction upon whaling led to concern about over-fishing. The International Whaling Commission was formed by interested nations and, acting upon scientific advice, set quotas to prevent the new intensive methods resulting in the extinction of species such as the blue whale. These quotas are difficult to enforce and should, when imposed, have resulted in the decline of factory ship whaling. The fact that Japan and Russia both operate factory fleets in the North Pacific indicates that these quotas are being exceeded.

Over-fishing is particularly dangerous for the sperm whale whose population dynamics are almost completely unknown. The main considerations are, of course, commercial and while there is demand for whale products in excess of the stipulated quotas over-fishing will continue.

The high demand for sperm whale oil fractions in the British soft-leather industry continues in the face of the need to conserve sperm whales, despite the fact that synthetic substitutes are available. The flagrant breaches of the agreements of the IWC, particularly by Japan, highlight the ineffectual nature of the Commission.

Of late, public awareness of the plight of the whale population has resulted in a ban on the use of whale products in the United States. This

The killer whale *Orcinus orca* (*above*) is often seen off northern Scotland in the summer, the characteristic black fins of a school cutting the water in formation. The pilot whale or blackfish *Globicephala melaena* (*below*) inhabits the North Atlantic and South Pacific in herds of several hundreds.

Pl. 4

Killer.
Pilot Whale

The common dolphin *Delphinus delphis* is found in temperate areas of the Atlantic and is common in the Bay of Biscay and the Mediterranean. Despite its size – it can grow to 2.1m in length and weigh up to 136kg – the dolphin has a friendly reputation, and will often play alongside a boat.

awareness, shared by many Britons, has no doubt stemmed from the media coverage given to the whales and the establishment of various oceanaria in both countries.

The bottlenosed dolphin *Tursiops truncatus* is perhaps the best known by virtue of its popularity as a performer in these establishments. It is fairly easy to catch and to keep alive once in captivity. The common dolphin *Delphinus delphis* is widely distributed and has been known since classical times. It has the enviable reputation of saving the lives of drowning men by pushing them ashore, but the truth of this is open to some doubt.

The killer whale *Orcinus orca*, despite its fearsome reputation, is also kept in oceanaria where it is found to be tractable and highly intelligent. There are many problems associated with maintaining such large animals as killer whales in oceanaria. Examination by a veterinarian soon after capture is essential and the treatment of any wounds incurred during capture is vital. Younger animals appear to be less hardy. The captured whale must be assisted in adapting to the new environment. Some dolphins and porpoises never satisfactorily adjust and must be released. Water quality is of paramount importance. Bacteria pose a substantial problem to all captive marine mammals and must be removed in a water-treatment programme. This is designed to deal also with water fouling, insecticides and toxic chemicals.

Much valuable information has been produced as a result of research on captive dolphins and porpoises. Many of the techniques for handling and transporting these animals are now routine. The fundamental requirement is for the animal to be kept moist and cool. The ability of many whales to communicate has been recognized and well documented as a result of research in oceanaria. Significant advances have been made in the fields of physiology and anatomy as well as in medical treatment of these animals.

Two male grey seals *Halichoerus grypus*, showing colour variation. Also known as the Atlantic seal, this offshore marine species comes ashore to breed. They frequent islands and rocky coasts, and usually stay close to the water's edge. Female grey seals are light grey or brown with darker spots.

Seals, Sealions and Walruses

Much of the pioneering work on the husbandry of captive marine mammals was performed upon another group: the seals, sealions and walruses or Pinnipedia. These animals are easier to keep in captivity by virtue of their amphibious nature: they spend considerable periods of time out of water and have thus adapted to both a terrestrial and an aquatic existence.

The Pinnipedia are a specialized group of carnivores, and fall naturally into two main divisions: the eared seals and the earless sealions. The walruses form a third group intermediate between the other two. The term 'earless' is misleading and describes the reduced ear pinnae of these sealions. Both groups have, in fact, functional ears. The earless seals are regarded as being more completely adapted for an aquatic existence.

Probably the best known of this group of animals is the Californian sealion *Eumetopius jubatus*. These are seen often in zoos and circuses and appear to have a natural ability for balancing objects on their snout. They thrive well in captivity, learn quickly and have long memories. In the wild they are active predators, feeding on squid and fish. Spiny fish are not eaten.

Of the two indigenous British species of seal,

A. Thorburn
1920

the grey seal *Halichoerus grypus* is the more common. Breeding grounds in this country are limited, but where they do occur the seals congregate and give birth on dry land. The white fur of the calves is often lost before birth. The same breeding colonies are frequented each year; after the breeding period the animals disperse.

The other British seal, the common seal *Phoca vitulina*, is, despite its name, rarer than the grey seal, at least on the west coast. This species is the victim of the ambivalent attitude of man to sea mammals in general. Large numbers of yearlings are hunted for their skins which make attractive, though stiff, coats. In Alaska they are shot in endeavours to protect the salmon for sport. Indeed, the alleged damage to commercial fisheries by seals led, in 1934, to the slaughter of 177 grey seals on the Cornish coast. Certainly the bad reputation which seals have among fishermen is exploited by the sealers in their arguments to increase cull numbers.

The harp seal *Pagophilus groenlandicus* has been the object of much public concern. Found in the North Atlantic, particularly on the East Canadian coast, the new born pups of this species are hunted for their white coats. The animals are clubbed to death to avoid damaging the pelts which are used for furs. The intervention of 'Greenpeace', the conservation organization, to impede the hunting took place in the late 1970s. Much publicity was given to the unpleasant killing methods and to the prepossessing appearance of the pups. The ringed seal *Pusa hispida* has six subspecies found in both the North Atlantic and Pacific Oceans. Many thousands are also taken annually, mainly for their skins.

In common with the whales, seals have many adaptations to aquatic life, although the actual mechanisms employed differ between the two groups. Blubber, however, is found in both seals and whales, and seal blubber is important to the Eskimos as a source of oil. All parts of the

Common seals *Phoca vitulina* are smaller and less gregarious than the grey seal. They are to be found all round the British coastline, but are rarer on the west coast. Their main food is flatfish, crustaceans and molluscs, on which they grow up to 2m.

The ringed seal *Pusa hispida* (*above*) and the harp seal *Pagophilus groenlandicus* (*below*). Both have suffered huge losses from culls and skin-hunting, but are still to be found in the circumpolar region; they live under the ice, maintaining holes in the surface where they can come up for breath. Rarely seen around Britain.

ringed seal are used by these people: the skins are used to cover kayaks and the liver and intestine are eaten either boiled or frozen. The bearded seal *Erignathus barbatus* is also very important to the Eskimo way of life. The strong hide is used to make boot soles and strong ropes, and is also used to feed sledge dogs. The intestine is eaten and sometimes used for window panes. The liver often contains a poisonous level of vitamin A and dogs will not eat it when it is fresh. The extensive blubber is either eaten or rendered down for lamp oil.

The hooded or bladdernosed seal *Cystophora cristata* derives its name from the inflatable reddish hood present on the head of the males. This may be inflated when the animal is angered.

The bearded seal *Erignathus barbatus* (*above*) and the hooded seal *Cystophora cristata* (*below*). Both species live in the Arctic. The fur of the young hooded seal is particularly sought after by hunters since, for the first year, it is pure white. In the region of 3000 hooded seals are slaughtered every year.

Another curious feature is the pliable nasal septum which is also red and may be extruded through one nostril. The function of this is unknown.

Another animal of bizarre appearance is the walrus *Odobenus rosmarus* immortalized in Lewis Carroll's poem *The Walrus and the Carpenter*. Although the creature feeds upon shellfish, these are not obtained by the playing of confidence tricks as upon the hapless oysters in the poem, but dug from the seabed using the tusks. Stomachs of the walrus containing shellfish of the species *Cardium groenlandicum* are regarded as a great delicacy by the Eskimos. The tears shed by Carroll's walrus, supposedly over the demise of the tricked oysters, were not a manifestation of grief but a phenomenon noted in many seals. Tears flow over the face, not because the eyes are irritated by air as is often stated, but because seals have no naso-lachrymal duct connecting the eyes and nasal passages. In other mammals, tears (which are continuously produced) are channelled through this duct into the nose.

Despite stringent limits imposed upon walrus catching in Alaska and Canada, their numbers continue to decline. It is to be hoped that this curious creature, now severely reduced in both the Atlantic and Pacific, will survive.

The application of a conservation policy to sea mammals in general is necessary as a result of their over-exploitation in the past. Whale numbers in particular have been seriously reduced, and hunting of the small species such as the sei whale *Balaenoptera borealis* has now begun. In the case of the seals, the dwindling number of suitable breeding grounds, as a result of the activities of man, poses a problem.

Properly managed, sea mammals constitute a valuable resource. They have an ability to concentrate the somewhat diffuse resources of the sea. To emulate this process man would need to apply considerable effort and ingenuity. Predictably, though, having over-fished the whale, the industry is now concentrating upon means of utilizing the whale's food, 'krill', directly. The regularly aired opinion that whales may be equivalent in intelligence to man is also worthy of consideration in our treatment of these animals.

The walrus *Odobenus rosmarus* lives in large herds in the circumpolar seas of North America and Europe. The long tusks, which grow to 1m in length, are used to dig up molluscs from rocks and shingle under the water, which are found by feeling with the highly sensitive, copious, quill-like whiskers.

Pl. 12.

Storm Petrel.
Frigate Petrel.
Wilson's Petrel.

Leach's Fork-tailed Petrel.
Madeiran Fork-tailed Petr
Sooty Shearwater.

Petrels and Shearwaters

Little was known about the distribution and breeding habits of the storm petrels until the recent studies made on Skokholm populations. Storm petrels are highly developed oceanic birds adapted to an aerial way of life. The small legs set well back mean that the birds shuffle on land and in their breeding burrows. These are either dug with the beak or are adopted puffin or rabbit burrows, and are usually set in cliffs or steep hillsides so minimizing difficulties in landing and taking off.

Of the five petrels illustrated by Thorburn the storm petrel *Hydrobates pelagicus* and the Leach's petrel *Oceanodroma leucorhoa* are resident and partial migrants; the others are vagrants usually brought by storms. Both species may be seen on clear moonlit nights, display-flying and calling to one another during the breeding season, but since they arrive after dusk and depart before dawn, many breeding sites along our western coasts and islands may well have been overlooked. Most observers tend to visit islands during the daylight hours when only adult birds are present in burrows, incubating the eggs. Even the great efforts of the Operation Seafarer Census in 1969 to 1971 did not manage to gain accurate estimates of numbers and colonies. When not incubating or feeding young, the petrels are out at sea feeding on small fish and planktonic shrimps which come to the sea's surface at night. Other items also found floating on the surface, such as faeces and animal debris, will be eaten too. Fully fed breeding birds re-appear one hour after dusk, and male and female alternate incubation at three-day intervals. Incubation will last for 40 days, a long time for such small birds. Fledglings depart within ten weeks.

The storm petrel, colloquially known as Mother Cary's Chicken, is the smallest of our seabirds, weighing 25 grams, despite a wing-span of 36 to 39 centimetres, while its well-fed chick and the Leach's petrel weigh double this. Although both breed in Britain, the northwest islands of Scotland are the easternmost outpost of the Leach's petrel, a Pacific and west Atlantic bird. The storm petrel is a northwest Atlantic bird during the breeding season and the British western coasts and isles are the major strongholds of its colonies.

The shearwaters are really petrels, though the Latin *Puffinus* often confuses these birds with those of the auk family to which the puffin belongs. Of the four shearwaters, only one – the Manx shearwater – breeds on British coasts. The great shearwater *Puffinus gravis* breeds in the Tristan da Cunha group of islands in the south Atlantic, after which it migrates to north Atlantic waters and commonly visits our western coasts between August and September. The little shearwater *P. assimilis* has, like the black-browed albatross *Diomedea melanophris*, been recorded in greater numbers since 1963; these British specimens have all come from the race in the east-central Atlantic. The sooty shearwater *P. griseus* has a wide circumpolar breeding distribution in the southern latitudes, but migrates to the northern oceans in spring. It is found at sea off northwest Europe from August to November, and sometimes non-breeding birds are seen until March.

The Manx shearwater *P. puffinus* breeds in the northern hemisphere and there are three distinct races in Europe: two in the Mediterranean and the third around our shores. The British population has been estimated at 300,000 breeding pairs, usually in large colonies. Nesting burrows are often communal and interconnect below ground. This shearwater's breeding and rearing habits are similar to those of the storm petrel. At the end of the breeding season all the birds return to the ocean with the main body of adults migrating to the east coast of South America.

Some of the birds illustrated in Thorburn's original work are now accepted as being improbable sights in Britain. The following four species

Clockwise from top left British storm petrel *Hydrobates pelagicus*, Leach's petrel *Oceanodroma leucorhoa*, Madeiran storm petrel *O. castro*, sooty shearwater *Puffinus griseus*, great shearwater *P. gravis*, little shearwater *P. assimilis*, Wilson's petrel *O. oceanicus*, frigate petrel *Pelagodroma marina*.

of petrels are rarely seen in the northwest Atlantic, let alone in Britain. First, the collared or Gould's petrel *Pterodroma leucoptera* occurs in the tropics and sub-tropics of the Pacific Ocean. One specimen was said to have been shot on the west Welsh coast in 1889. Second, Kermadec's petrel *P. neglecta* is also Pacific, and the specimen found dead in Cheshire in 1908 was a long way off its normal haunts around the Tuamotu Archipelago in the south Pacific. Third, a rare sight, the capped petrel or Diablotin *P. hasitata* has been recently discovered breeding in the Carribean. It is a rare vagrant to the United States. The fourth petrel has three records from Britain and Ireland over the last 150 years. This is Bulwer's petrel *Bulweria bulwerii* which has a relict worldwide distribution and in the Atlantic is found breeding on the islands west of north Africa and Portugal.

Since 1963 there has been a spate of records of the black-browed albatross. This large bird has a 200 to 250 centimetre wingspan and, therefore, cannot be easily confused with the smaller gannet with which it tends to be seen. It breeds on islands between 60°S and 20°S in the Atlantic and sometimes may have flown to Britain by following ships.

Fulmar

The fulmar *Fulmaris glacialis* is now almost as familiar as the gulls around northern waters. This elegant bird with a wingspan of 100 to 110 centimetres now graces the wake of trawlers, harbour fish-landings and sewage outlets in the cold waters of northwest Europe.

The fulmar has three races in the north Pacific and Atlantic, and St Kilda was an outpost for the larger-billed Atlantic race. These ancient colonies had been harvested by the islanders and Vikings for 1000 years until the evacuation of Hirta in 1930. The island's export economy was primarily based on fulmars for oil and feathers, and on sheep for wool, but the yearly cull of eggs and adult fulmars never exterminated this species in the way that culls did other birds on such islands as the Faroes. Since the evacuation, the colony has peaked at 40,000 occupied nest sites per year.

The fulmar's colonization of Europe began in 1753 when it was first recorded in Iceland. In 1839 the Faroes became a breeding ground; north Britain followed in 1878 and then Norway in 1924. By 1969 to 1970 the European population had reached 305,000, with all but a few thousand in Britain, Ireland and on St Kilda.

Clockwise from top left Black-browed albatross *Diomedea melanophris*, Manx shearwater *Puffinus puffinus*, capped petrel *Pterodroma hasitata*, Bulwer's petrel *Bulweria bulwerii*, Kermadec petrel *Pterodroma neglecta*, fulmar *Fulmarus glacialis*, Gould's or collared petrel *Pterodroma leucoptera*.

Pl. 8

lack browed Albatross. (scale ½)
Manx Shearwater.
Capped Petrel.
Collared Petrel.
Bulwer's Petrel.
Fulmar

Diving seabirds

Last century the gannet or Solan goose *Sula bassana* was ruthlessly exploited by man for food and feathers. The famous Bird Rocks colony in the Gulf of St Lawrence was decimated from 110,000 pairs in 1829 to a handful by 1894. The depredations by man in Britain were curtailed by the introduction of the Protection of Seabirds Act in 1869, and now the gannet receives protection throughout its range. The British population numbered 142,000 pairs in 1969 to 1970, a three-fold increase since the 1910s. Before the Seabirds Act, the Bass Rock colony in the Firth of Forth provided birds for the Edinburgh market, costing two shillings and fourpence each – the same price as in the early 1700s. The St Kilda people used to take 20,000 gannets a year for local consumption, besides fulmars, puffins and auks.

Thorburn illustrates the nestling and juvenile in grey plumage. The bird diving is sub-adult: it has not yet lost all its juvenile black. Over four years of erratic moulting, the plumage gradually changes until the adult white breeding coloration is attained. The thick padded feathers on the throat and chest and the strengthened bone structure absorb much of the impact during the dives, often from heights of 10 to 40 metres down to a depth of 15 metres. The gannet's diet of surface-shoaling mackerel and herring are always eaten whole before the bird rises for another dive. Offal is taken when available. A pair of gannets lay and rear a single chick which is fed on semi-digested food regurgitated by the parents.

In contrast to the gannets, the cormorant *Phalacrocorax carbo* and shag *P. aristotelis* dive from the water surface, sometimes with a small forward leap. Like the freshwater grebes, the feet are used for forward propulsion and the wings are held tightly against the body. Studies on the cormorant show that although its diet is chiefly fish, in the southwest of England only ten per cent of the fish caught was of marketable value. In lochs, inland waterways and tidal rivers, brown trout may form a substantial proportion of fish caught, though human presence tends to keep these birds away. Predominantly bottom-dwelling fish are taken, whereas shags take mainly middle-water fish. Consequently, shags are more often seen feeding close to shore and in estuaries where the water's depth is less than ten metres. The English used to train cormorants to fish, and the Chinese still do.

Both these birds nest colonially on ledges and rocky cliffs. In Ireland cormorants will nest in trees inland, if there are adequate feeding grounds. The larger and better made the nest, the higher the survival rate of young and eggs, since falling off the nest ledges is a common fate. The shag favours more sheltered and shaded sites for nests than the cormorant which inhabits the more exposed sites.

The relaxation of persecution of the shags by fishermen has resulted in a marked increase along the northeast coast of England since the turn of the century; in the period 1905 to 1965 the number of pairs rose from 10 to 1900 but numbers have remained fairly constant over Britain as a whole, with the total population at over 30,000 pairs. The cormorants suffered heavily in the last century all over Britain and the Continent, and are still declining due to deaths from pollution by oil and other wastes particularly accumulations of pesticides and polychlorinated biphenyls (PCBs) from industry. The British population stood at around 8000 pairs in 1969 to 1970.

A colony of gannets *Sula bassana* (*top*), showing young birds with their brown plumage as well as the adult birds. A cormorant *Phalacrocorax carbo* (*below left*) with its young; the plumage is not oiled as in other species. A shag *P. aristotelis* (*below right*) with young.

Gannet. (adults & young)

Cormorant (adult & young) Shag

Black Guillemot. (summer & winter).
Common Guillemot.
Razorbill (summer & winter
Puffin. (summer & winter).
Brünnick's Guille

Auks

It is probable that several tens of thousands of seabirds have died annually during the last 30 years from oil pollution around the British coasts. The Torre Canyon disaster accounted for the death of huge numbers of guillemots and brought to the fore this problem which grows every year with the increasing oil-tanker traffic and the North Sea oilfields. The recent spate of oil disasters has affected especially all members of the auk family for, when polluted, the auks repeatedly duck under the water to rid themselves of the new 'black death', only to end up by covering themselves with even more oil. Gulls and other birds usually fly away. The earlier view that it was virtually impossible to save an oiled seabird has been modified by recent research; but the process requires much time and care.

The flightless great auk *Pinguinus impennis* became extinct through over-hunting, a volcanic eruption and, finally, through specimen collectors taking the world's last surviving pair in 1844. At present, the other auks are not in danger of this fate, but complacency has been the cause of many extinctions. Both the guillemot *Uria aalge* and puffin *Fratercula arctica* have suffered severe declines in population but these are not due to the lack of protection from man's hunting and trapping. Their numbers probably exceed half a million pairs each, but exact counting is impractical. Individual colonies in southwest England, the Irish Sea and southwest Scotland have suffered most of the decreases. Many northwestern colonies had never been surveyed before the Operation Seafarer census of 1969 to 1970, but even these seem to be decreasing at an alarming rate, despite the vast numbers of birds seen on a cursory inspection.

In some islands it appears that the effect of the brown rat preying on chicks and eggs, and other factors such as predation by gulls, and land erosion in the case of burrow-nesting species are causing this decline. Adult mortality becomes very important when the reproductive rate of a bird species is only one chick per pair each year. A single oil spill has the same effect as collecting up to 75 per cent of the eggs over 50 years. This is, of course, only one side of the story: climatic changes over the long term and subsequent differences in food supply in either winter or summer grounds cannot be so easily evaluated, and represent an unknown factor in long-term bird ecology.

Of the other auk species, both the little auk *Alle alle* and Brünnich's or the arctic guillemot *Uria lomvia* are vagrants to Britain's northern shores, records of the latter numbering half a dozen this century. The little auk occasionally appears widespread across Britain, driven here by prolonged cyclones from its wintering grounds in the north Atlantic.

Clockwise from top left black guillemot or Tystie *Cepphus grylle*, common guillemot *Uria aalge*, puffin *Fratercula arctica*, Brünnich's or arctic guillemot *Uria lomvia*, little auk *Alle alle*, great auk *Pinguinus impennis* (now extinct) and razorbill *Alca torda*.

Terns

The arrival of the terns to the shores of Britain heralds the summer, just as the martins and swallows do inland. With their long, forked tail feathers and graceful flight they have been named the 'swallows of the sea'. It is curious that two unrelated groups of birds have evolved such similarities. Both are migratory, breeding in the arctic and temperate summers and generally wintering in the tropics or sub-tropics of the southern continents.

Of the 13 species of terns recorded in Britain, only five breed here regularly: the common *Sterna hirundo*, arctic *S. paradisaea*, Sandwich *S. sandvicensis*, roseate *S. dougallii* and little *S. albifrons*. Five others are rare vagrants from other continents and two are annual vagrants from eastern Europe and Asia. The last, the black tern *S. niger* is now a passage migrant – in contrast to early last century when it bred regularly in the Fenlands. This was the only exclusively inland, water-inhabiting tern in England but, along with the great crested grebe, it had ceased breeding in the Fens by 1855.

The nests are simple, usually consisting of no more than a shallow depression in the sand or shingle occasionally lined with a few stray weed stems or twigs. Some protection of the eggs is afforded by their camouflage colouring that blends in with the sand and shingle. The nest, or scrape, of the little tern is made on a beach and is often so shallow that the eggs may be blown away during gales or taken by ever-watchful gulls. In the open nesting sites of terns, predation by herring gulls on the chicks and eggs can sometimes cause heavy losses or local extinctions of common terns, as happened at Vlieland in the Friesans. The presence of such gulleries, however, may provide Sandwich terneries with protection from skuas and other large seabirds. The major problem with terneries today is disruption and interference by man. The main breeding sites are currently under the protection of various bird trusts, especially in Norfolk which is a main stronghold of the common, Sandwich and little terns.

The arctic tern is easily mistaken for the common tern, but close inspection will reveal that the bill of the arctic tern is blood-red but, unlike the common tern, it lacks a black tip. It has a more northerly range than the common tern, and breeding sites extend from Norfolk to 83°N in Greenland. Its wintering grounds reach further south than those of other terns, towards 80°S in the Antarctic where the related and sedentary antarctic tern *S. vittata* dwells. A round trip of 30,000 kilometres a year makes the arctic tern the greatest of all migratory birds. Like other terns and many seabirds, the arctic tern does not breed until its third year and reaches its maximum breeding rate by its tenth. Egg clutches are small and each pair of adults will rear only one or two chicks in a good year. This longevity is a common feature of many British seabirds and allows survival of the species despite a series of breeding season failures.

The behavioural patterns of terns are easily observed and provide much interest to the amateur watcher. Disturbance of a colony will cause the birds to fly noisily up *en masse*, a phenomenon known as a 'dread'. Anyone disturbing a nesting arctic tern receives a nasty shock; one may be dive-bombed and mocked. But the weaker cries of the little tern are usually ignored as one stumbles across its nest on a deserted beach.

Above A tern on the Moray Firth in August; a large flock had gathered on the shore before migrating southwards.
Opposite (*clockwise from top left*) roseate tern *Sterna dougallii*, arctic tern *S. paradisaea*, common tern *S. hirundo*, little tern *S. albifrons* and sandwich tern *S. sandvicensis*.

Pl. 71.

Roseate Tern. Arctic Tern.

Common Tern.

A. Thorburn 1915.
Herring Gull. (adult & young).
Lesser Black-backed Gull.

Gulls

The success of gulls in colonizing new habitats is especially marked around urban developments. At least 200,000 blackheaded gulls *Larus ridibundus* can be found in winter on the reservoirs and gravel pits in the London area. This scavenging gull started spreading from coastal areas at the turn of the century and has now become a common sight in many cities. The presence of food in the large urban waste tips is now as much a food source as worms from newly ploughed farmland or fish offal from trawlers. Breeding colonies are found in both coastal dunes and marshes and on inland moors, hill lochs and sometimes sewage farms.

Opposite (*clockwise from top left*) herring gull *Larus argentatus*, lesser black-backed *L. fuscus*, great black-headed *L. ichthyaetus*, and Iceland *L. glaucoides*.
Below Great black-backed gull *L. marinus* (*top*), ringed plover *Charadrius hiaticula* (*left*) and turnstone *Arenaria interpres* (*right*).

The Mediterranean gull *L. melanocephalus* is often mistaken for the similar blackheaded gull although it lacks the black wing tips. Recently, this common winter visitor has been seen increasingly in the south and east of England, and is breeding in western Europe, sometimes hybridizing with the blackheaded gull. The expansion of the Mediterranean gull from its Aegean and Black Sea breeding grounds is a reflection of the spread of gulls generally.

The herring gull *L. argentatus* and, more recently, the kittiwake *Rissa tridactyla*, have both increased dramatically in numbers and range. This is most probably due to the greatly increased food supply from man in winter. This opportunistic family of birds is similar to the pigeons and doves in adaptability, and ability to colonize new habitats quickly.

The presence of different races of gulls indicates a currently evolving group. Both the herring gull and the lesser black-backed gull *L. fuscus* exist as two species in northern Europe, and hybridi-

zation with fertile offspring can occur between them. Generally these two birds nest in separate colonies. Increasingly though they are found together around the coasts and towns of Britain, scavenging for refuse, carrion, and offal in winter. During the breeding season the lesser black-backed and herring gulls tend to feed on their normal diet of birds, eggs, fish and invertebrates and return to their coastal, cliff and moorland colonies.

The behaviour of gulls has been immortalized in Niko Tinbergen's *A Herring Gull's World*. Such a book illustrates how much there is to discover about even the commonest of our birds. The gulls provided a vast field of new work for both amateur and professional biologists, a more worthwhile occupation than that of the Victorian specimen hunters.

Some of the gulls Thorburn illustrates are rare visitors or vagrants. Arctic breeding gulls are more often found around the northern shores and islands of Britain, such as the glaucous gull *L. hyperboreus*, the pure white ivory gull *Pagophila eburnea* and Sabine's gull *L. sabini*. The smallest gull of all, the little gull *L. minutus*, is a regular passage migrant and a visitor in varying numbers to Scotland and the south and east coasts of England.

The 1960s showed an increase of 50 per cent in the number of breeding kittiwakes to an estimated half a million breeding pairs in 1969 to 1970. Until then, no reliable national counts of kittiwakes had been made and the population explosion had not been confirmed. It is an oceanic gull during the winter when it is found in the North Atlantic. Breeding adults arrive at British coasts from late winter, nest on cliff-ledges, and depart between late summer and early the next winter.

This small gull supplied eggs, decorative feathers and sport to the Victorians before the protection laws were enacted 90 years ago. Since then it is probable that populations expanded at the rate of 50 percent per ten years, but within the existing colonies; this was unlike the fulmar which formed new colonies, thereby drawing attention to its expansion.

The small number of predatory great skuas do not affect the vast number of kittiwakes in Scotland; probably two-thirds of all kittiwakes are centred around Shetland, Orkney and Caithness. It will be interesting to see if this expansion around the British coast continues.

Above Male (*top*) and female smew *Mergus albellus*. This duck is a winter visitor to the British Isles.
Opposite Kittiwake *Rissa tridactyla* (*top*), great black-backed gull *Larus marinus* adult and young (*centre*), ivory gull *Pagophila eburnea* (*bottom left*) and glaucous gull.

A. Thorburn
1915
Kittiwake Gull (adult & young).
Great Black-backed Gull (adult & young).

Harlequin Duck (♂ ♀)

Eider Duck. (♂ ♀)

King-Eider. (♂ ♀)

Sea Ducks

The sea ducks: the eiders, scoters and mergansers, all share sexual dimorphism of the breeding plumage, which is a characteristic feature of all ducks. Nests are usually made from local plant stems, and are always lined with down taken from the female's breast.

The eider duck *Somateria mollissima* is the best known of the British sea ducks, and regularly breeds around the northern shores and islands. The current population of from 15,000 to 25,000 pairs is gradually spreading, and they are already breeding as far south as Walney in Cumbria. In winter many migrant eider arrive, and the characteristic rafts of the black and white drakes may be seen offshore.

Like the other sea ducks, the eider breeds in the sub-arctic and arctic regions, forming large colonies on islands in the protection of bays and promontories. This has been exploited over many centuries by the Icelanders and Faroese who encourage the ducks to settle and harvest the down, so famous for its thermal insulation. Indeed, this down provides adequate protection from egg chilling when nests are made on frozen ground. The female incubates the clutch, without ever leaving the nest. As soon as the young hatch they take to the sea, where often they are tended in nurseries by both the mothers and 'aunts' or non-breeding females. The gregariousness of these and other ducks seems to provide protection from predatory gulls, skuas and seals. Like scoters, they commonly dive for shellfish and crustacean food. The eider may dive three or six metres down; the related long-tailed duck, however, may dive down to 48 metres.

The common scoter *Melanitta nigra* is a regular winter resident on our southern and eastern coasts. This dark coloured sea duck breeds very locally in the north of both Britain and Ireland, though many non-breeding birds will summer off the western coasts. Unlike eiders, the scoter nests inland, usually in the tundra and boreal zones around the arctic. In summer, its diet is predominantly freshwater insects, larvae, crustacea and plant material, but this diet changes to shellfish on arrival at the marine winter grounds.

The velvet scoter *M. fusca* regularly winters off our east coasts. It tends to keep offshore and is often imperceptible among flocks of common scoter.

Both the surf scoter *M. perspicillata* and Steller's eider *Polystica stelleri* are rare winter vagrants. The king eider *Somataria spectabilis* winters further north than the eider at the limits of the ice, but may be seen off the north of Scotland when ice and weather are severe.

Opposite Sea ducks, with males in breeding plumage and the more sombre females: harlequin *Histrionicus histrionicus (top)*, eider *Somateria mollissima (centre)* and king eider *Somateria spectabilis (bottom)*.
Below A sketch of the eider duck. Their nests provide the down which are used to stuff pillows and quilts.

Waders

Britain's coasts, estuaries and wetlands with their mild maritime climate provide a wide range of habitats and food resources that are annually exploited by over 50 species of waders. This large group of birds includes the plovers, sandpipers, curlews, godwits, phalaropes and the avocet. The diversity of adaptations to feeding on shellfish, shrimps, seaworms and mud is easily seen in the variety of shapes and sizes in bills and legs. The vast flocks of over-wintering birds seen on the eastern shores account for only a fraction of one per cent of the yearly growth of marine mud and sand-dwelling organisms.

In the nesting waders, four main types of site are selected. Open sites with minimal, low ground-cover provide a good view of predators and other birds. The lapwings, avocets, ringed plovers, little ringed plovers, dotterels and oystercatchers choose these, and make a simple scrape in the bare sand, shingle or short grass. Curlews, whimbrels and golden plovers select a tuft of grass that protects one side of the nest, also the function of the piece of debris or wood adopted by the greenshank. Finally, nests may be hidden inside close vegetation and grass as those of black-tailed godwits, red-necked phalaropes, redshank, snipe, dunlin and sandpipers.

Both sexes may be involved in nest site selection, the male often making several scrapes, but in the red-necked phalarope *Phalaropus lobatus* it is the female which has the more brightly coloured plumage, chooses the nesting territory and attracts the male. The ruff shows the opposite extreme with the male sporting an enormous erectile ruff and ear tufts during spring courtship displays to which the females, the reeves, are attracted. Although a successful male will mate with many females, he will not take part in nestbuilding, incubation or the rearing of young.

The oystercatcher *Haematopus ostralegus* performs a curious 'piping' display contagious to other oystercatchers. When excited, after a territorial encounter or courtship, the bird will run up and down the beach with its sideways flattened beak partly opened and pointed downwards. This piping noise attracts others so that in a few minutes a dozen or more may be seen performing this curious display. Avocets *Recurvirostra avosetta* are easily recognized by their black and white plumage and unique, upwardly curved bill. Though they became extinct during last century after their wetland haunts were drained, over the last 30 years they have become re-established in East Anglia. They occasionally perform a ritualized behaviour, of perhaps social origin, that is termed 'grouping'. A group of birds will form a circle and bow with heads and bills held low in the centre. Afterwards, a closely associated male and female may show aggressive behaviour towards other pairs in the group.

During the autumn, many waders which breed in the arctic tundra arrive on our shores,

Opposite (*clockwise from top left*) Grey phalaropes *Phalaropus fulicarius*, oystercatcher *Haematopus ostralegus*, avocet *Recurvirostra avosetta*, red-necked phalarope *P. lobatus*, black-winged stilt *Himantopus himantopus* and turnstone *Arenaria interpres*.

Left The avocet breeds in eastern and winters in western England.

Grey Phalarope. (winter & summer).
Turnstone. (summer & winter).

Oyster catcher. (summer & winter).
Avocet.

Black-winged Pratincole. Pratincole.
Caspian Plover. (adult & young). Cream-coloured Courser.
Ringed Plover.

Opposite (*clockwise from top left*) Black-winged pratincole *Glareola nordmanni*, collared pratincole *G. pratincola*, cream courser *Cursori cursor*, ringed plover *Charadrius hiaticula*, Kentish plover *C. alexandrius*, little plover *C. dubius*, dotterel *Endromia morinillus* and Caspian plover *C. asiaticus*.
Above Golden plover *Pluvialis apricaria*, grey plover *P. squatarola* and curlew *Numenius arquata* (with curved bill).

among them jack snipe, ruffs, purple sandpipers, little stints and bar-tailed godwits. The early arrival of some lapwings and green sandpipers is due to their not having bred successfully in their northern grounds. These return well before the majority in July and August. Flocks of lapwings, dunlin and knot may roost or fly together but, like other waders, the different species tend to feed separately.

Flocking of many birds provides added protection against predators when either feeding at low tide or resting at high tide. The development of white flashes and bars is strong in these communal waders and appears to act as flock markers and signals.

Books illustrated by Thorburn's Plates

In the following alphabetical-by-author list of books illustrated by Thorburn, and of some later books in which his plates have been reproduced, the year or years cited are those of the first edition unless otherwise indicated.

Anker, Jean, *Bird Books and Bird Art: An Outline of the History and Iconography of Descriptive Ornithology*. Levin and Munksgaard, Copenhagen, 1938.

Archer, Sir Geoffrey Francis and Godman, Eva Mary, *The Birds of British Somaliland and the Gulf of Aden*. Gurney & Jackson, London, 1937 (vols 1 and 2); Oliver & Boyd, London, 1937 (vols 3 and 4). Contains Thorburn's last published plates.

Beebe, C. W., *A Monograph of the Pheasants*. Witherby, London; 4 vols, 1918–22. Some of the finest of the 90 colour plates are by Thorburn.

Benson, S. Vere, *The Observer's Book of British Birds*. Warne, London, 1937. Contains many Thorburn plates from Lilford (1885–98).

Brander, Michael (Ed.), *The International Encyclopedia of Shooting*. Pelham, London, 1972. Contains a Thorburn plate of blackcock.

Buxton, Sydney Charles [Earl Buxton], *Fishing and Shooting*. John Murray, London, 1902.

Coward, T. A., *The Birds of the British Isles and Their Eggs*. Warne, London, 1920–6; 3 vols. Contains many Thorburn plates from Lilford (1885–98).

Coward, T. A., *Bird Haunts and Nature Memories*. Warne, London, 1922. Contains a fine Thorburn frontispiece of a noctule, dated 10 October 1919.

Coward, T. A., *Bird Life At Home and Abroad with Other Nature Observations*. Warne, London and New York, 1927.

Dale, Thomas Francis, *The Fox*. Longmans, Green & Co., London, 1906 (*Fur, Feather and Fin Series, no. 12*).

Dewar, George Albermarle Bertie, *Life and Sport in Hampshire*. Longmans, Green & Co., London, 1908. Includes two colour plates by Thorburn.

Dresser, Henry Eeles, Sharpe, Richard Bowdler and Hay, Arthur Viscount Walden, *A History of the Birds in Europe, Including all the Species Inhabiting the Western Palaearctic Region*. Published by the author, London; 9 vols including supplement, originally published in 93 parts 1871–81, 1895–6.

[Drewitt, C. M.,] *Lord Lilford . . . A Memoir by His Sister* [Hon. Mrs F. Dawtrey Drewitt]. Smith Elder, London, 1900. Includes seven plates in monochrome by Thorburn of Lilford Hall, Northamptonshire, and living birds in its aviaries.

Fisher, James, *Thorburn's Birds*. Michael Joseph, London, 1967. Includes 82 plates from Thorburn (1915–16).

Gladstone, H. S., *Handbook to Lord Lilford's Coloured Figures of the Birds of the British Islands*. Bickers, London, 1917.

Grimble, Augustus, *The Deer Forests of Scotland*. Kegan Paul & Co., London, 1896. Eight monochrome illustrations are by Thorburn.

Grimble, Augustus, *Deer-Stalking and the Deer Forests of Scotland*. Kegan Paul & Co., London, 1901. Eight monochrome illustrations are by Thorburn.

Grimble, Augustus, *Highland Sport*. Chapman & Hall, London, 1894.

Grimble, Augustus, *The Salmon Rivers of Scotland*. Kegan Paul & Co., London, 1902.

Grimble, Augustus, *Shooting and Salmon Fishing and Highland Sport*. Kegan Paul & Co., London,

1902. Contains 16 minochrome illustrations by Thorburn.

Hardy [Gathorne-Hardy], Hon. Alfred Erskine, *Autumns in Argylshire with Rod and Gun*. Longmans, Green & Co., London, 1900.

Harting, James Edmund, *Sketches of Bird Life*. Allen & Co., London, 1883. Two monochrome plates by Thorburn: the first to be published.

Harting, James Edmund, *The Rabbit*. Longmans, Green & Co., London, 1898 (*Fur, Feather and Fin Series*, no. 6). Monochrome frontispiece is by Thorburn.

Hudson, William Henry, and Beddard, Frank E., *British Birds*. Longmans, Green & Co., London, 1895. Eight coloured plates are by Thorburn.

Irby, L. Howard L., *The Ornithology of the Straits of Gibraltar*. Poter, London, 2nd ed. 1895. Eight colour plates are by Thorburn.

Koenig, A. [F.], *Avifauna Spitzbergensis. . . .* Published by the author, Bonn, 1911. Colour frontispiece was painted by Thorburn in 1910.

Lakatos, Károly, *A Vadászmesterseg Könyve*. Budapest, 1902.

Lilford, Baron [Thomas Little Powys], *Coloured Figures of the Birds of the British Islands*. Porter, London, 1885–98; 36 parts in 7 vols. Thorburn was brought in to the work of illustration in January 1887 and his first plate was published in part 7, vol. 2 in September 1888. He finally did the bulk of the work, 268 colour plates of the total of 421.

Lilford, Baron [Thomas Littleton Powys], *Notes on the Birds of Northamptonshire and Neighbourhood*. Porter, London, 1895; 2 vols. Contains 24 monochrome plates of birds and Northamptonshire scenery by Thorburn.

Little, Alicia Bewicke [Mrs Archibald], *Our Pet Herons*. Roy. Soc. Protect. Birds Leafl. no. 35. Contains Thorburn monochrome drawing of little egrets.

MacPherson, H. A. and others, *The Partridge*. Longmans, Green & Co., London, 1893 (*Fur and Feather Series*, no. 1). Nine monochrome plates are by Thorburn.

MacPherson, H. A. and others, *The Grouse*. Longmans, Green & Co., London, 1894 (*Fur and Feather Series*, no. 2). Ten monochrome plates and one vignette are by Thorburn.

MacPherson, H. A. and others, *The Pheasant*. Longmans, Green & Co., London, 1894 (*Fur and Feather Series*, no. 3). Nine plates (ten in 2nd edition, 1896) and one vignette, in monochrome, are by Thorburn.

MacPherson, H. A. and others, *The Hare*. Longmans, Green & Co., London, 1906 (*Fur and Feather Series*, no. 4). Three monochrome plates are by Thorburn.

MacPerson, H. A. and others, *The Red Deer*. Longmans, Green & Co., London, 1896 (*Fur and Feather Series*, no. 5). Six monochrome plates are by Thorburn.

Matschie, Paul, *Bilder aus dem Tierleben*. Union, Stuttgart, 1900.

Millais, John Guille, *The Natural History of the British Surface-Feeding Ducks*. Longmans, Green & Co., London, 1902. Eight colour plates are by Thorburn.

Millais, John Guille, *The Mammals of Great Britain and Ireland*. Longmans, Green & Co., London, 1904–6; 3 vols. Contains 30 colour plates by Thorburn done between 1893 and 1905.

Millais, John Guille, *The Natural History of the British Game Birds*. Longmans, Green & Co., London, 1909. Some of the 18 colour plates are by Thorburn.

Millais, John Guille, *British Diving Ducks*. Longmans, Green & Co., London, 1913; 2 vols. Contains 15 colour plates by Thorburn.

Millais, John Guille, *Rhododendrons*. Longmans, Green & Co., London, 1917, 1924; 2 vols. Contains two colour plates by Thorburn.

Millais, John Guille and others, *British Gamebirds and Wildfowl*, London, 1912 (*The Gun at Home and Abroad*); 2 vols. Some of the illustrations are by Thorburn.

Owen, J. A., 'The Lilford Vivaria'. *Pall Mall Mag.* 48–61, September 1896. Contains six monochrome illustrations by Thorburn.

Peek, Hedley, *The Poetry of Sport*. Longmans, Green & Co., London, 1885 (*Badminton Library*). Some of the illustrations are by Thorburn.

Powys, Thomas Littleton see Lilford

Pycraft, W. P., *Birds of Great Britain and Their Natural History*. Williams and Norgate, London, 1934. Colour frontispiece by Thorburn from Husson and Beddard, 1895.

Shaw, L. H. de Visme and others, *Snipe and Woodcock*. Longmans, Green & Co., London, 1903 (*Fur, Feather and Fin Series*, no. 10). Contains four monochrome plates by Thorburn.

Sitwell, Sacheverell, Buchanan, Handasyde and Fisher, James, *Fine Bird Books 1700–1900*. Collins, London, and Van Nostrand, New York, 1953.

Stewart, Henry Elliott, *The Birds of Our Country*, Digby & Long, London, 1897.

Swaysland, Walter, *Familiar Wild Birds*. Cassell & Co., London, 1883–8; 4 vols. Contains 144 coloured lithographs by Thorburn, his first major publishing assignment.

Trevor-Battye, A. (Ed.), *Lord Lilford on Birds*, Hutchinson & Co., London, 1903.

Thorburn, Archibald, 'Sabine's Gull in Cornwall'. *Zoologist*, 475–6.

Thorburn, Archibald, *British Birds*. Longmans, Green & Co., London, 1915–18; 4 vols. Contains 80 plates in colour, showing over 400 species.

Thorburn, Archibald, *A Naturalist's Sketch Book*. Longmans, Green & Co., London, 1919. Contains 60 plates, 24 in colour.

Thorburn, Archibald, *British Mammals*. Longmans, Green & Co., London, 1920–1; 2 vols. Contains 50 colour plates. The basis of the present book.

Thorburn, Archibald, *Game Birds and Wild-Fowl of Great Britain and Ireland*. Longmans, Green & Co., London, 1923. Contains 30 colour plates.

Thorburn, Archibald, *British Birds*. Longmans, Green & Co., London, 1925–6; 4 vols. Bibliographically the fourth edition of Thorburn (1915–18) with an octavo format and 192 new colour plates by the author.

Thorburn, Archibald, 'Kittiwakes nesting in Dunbar'. *Scot. Nat.* 1935 (212): 50. Thorburn's last published material and one of his few contributions to a scientific journal.

Further Reading

Alexander, H. G., *Seventy Years of Birdwatching*. Poyser, Berkhamstead, 1974.

Barrett-Hamilton, G. E. H. and Hinton, M. A. C., *A History of British Mammals*. Oliver-Boyd, Edinburgh, 1910–21; 2 vols.

Bell, T., *A History of British Quadrupeds*. John Van Voorst, London, 2nd ed. 1874.

Book of British Birds. Readers Digest Association and Automobile Association, Drive Publications, London, 1977.

Brink, F. H. van den, *A Field Guide to the Mammals of Britain and Europe*. Collins, London, 1967.

Brown, L., *British Birds of Prey*. Collins New Naturalist, London, 1976.

Burton, Maurice (Ed.), *The Shell History of Britain*. Michael Joseph, London, 1970.

Corbet, G. B., *The Identification of British Mammals*. British Museum (Natural History), London, 1964.

Cramp, S., Bourne, W. R. P., Saunders, D., *The Seabirds of Britain and Ireland*. Collins, London, 1974.

Cramp, S. and others, *The Birds of the Western Palaearctic*. Oxford University Press, Oxford, vol. I, 1977.

Crowcroft, P., *The Life of the Shrew*. Reinhardt, London, 1957.

Elliston, D., *The Naturalist in Britain*. Allen Lane, London, 1976.

Fisher, J. (Ed.), *A Journal of Natural History*, Collins New Naturalist, London, 1948.

Gibbs, J. A., *A Cotswold Village*. John Murray, London, 1898.

Goldsmith, O., *A History of Earth and Animated Nature*. Blackie, London, new ed. 1873; 2 vols.

Harrison, R. J. and King, J. E., *Marine Animals*. Hutchinson, London, 1965.

Hawksworth, D. L. (Ed.), *The Changing Fauna and Flora of Britain*. (Systematics Association, special vol. no. 6), Academic Press, London, 1974.

Hyams, E., *The Changing Face of Britain*. Kestrel Books, London, 1974.

Jefferies, R., *Wildlife in a Southern County*. Smith Elder, London, 1903.

Johns, Rev. C. A., *British Birds in their Haunts*. Routledge, London; revised by J. A. Owen, 1909.

Lawrence, M. J. and Brown, R. N., *Mammals of Britain, Their Tracks, Trails and Signs*. Blandford Press, London, revised ed. 1973.

Kearton, R., *With Nature and a Camera*. Cassell, London, 1897.

MacKenzie, O. H., *A Hundred Years in the Highlands*. Bles, London, 1952.

Matthews, L. H., *British Mammals*. Collins, London, 1952.

Mellanby, K., *The Mole*. Collins New Naturalist, London, 1971.

Millais, J. G., *The Mammals of Great Britain and Ireland*. Longmans, Green & Co., London, 1904–6; 3 vols.

Page, F. H. T., *Field Guide to British Deer*. Mammal Society of the British Isles, 1957.

Parslow, J., *Breeding Birds of Britain and Ireland*. Poyser, Berkhamstead, 1973.

Perry, R., *Wildlife in Britain and Ireland*. Croom Helm, London, 1978.

Peterson, R., Mountfort, G., Hollom, P. A. D., *A Field Guide to the Birds of Britain and Europe.* Collins, London, revised ed. 1974.

Phillips, W. A. A. and Blackmore, M., 'Mouse-eared Bats *Myotis myotis* in Sussex'. *Notes from the Mammal Society* no. 21, *J. Zool., Lond.* 1969; vol. 162, p. 4.

Racey, P. A. and Stebbings, R. E., 'Bats in Britain – A Status Report'. *Oryx*, 1972; vol. 11, no. 5, p. 319.

Sanders, E., *A Beast Book for the Pocket*. Oxford University Press, London, 1937.

Southern, H. N. (Ed.), *The Handbook of British Mammals*, Blackwell, Oxford, revised ed. 1965.

Stebbins, R. E., 'The Identification and Distribution of Bats of the Genus *Plecotus* in England'. *J. Zool.*, London, 1967; vol. 153, p. 291.

Street, P., *Mammals in the British Isles*. Robert Hale, London, 1961.

Tinbergen, Niko, *The Herring Gull's World.* Collins New Naturalist, London, 1953.

Vesey-Fitzgerald, B., *British Bats.* Methuen, London, 1949.

White, Gilbert, *The Natural History of Selbourne.* Frazer, Edinburgh, 2nd ed. 1838.

Whitehead, G. K., *The Deer of Great Britain and Ireland.* Routledge and Keegan Paul, London, 1964.

Index